Theresa M. Senft

CAMGIRLS

Celebrity & Community in the Age of Social Networks

PETER LANG

New York • Washington, D.C./Baltimore • Bern
Frankfurt am Main • Berlin • Brussels • Vienna • Oxford

Library of Congress Cataloging-in-Publication Data

Senft, Theresa M.
Camgirls: celebrity and community in the age of social networks /
Theresa M. Senft.
p. cm. — (Digital formations ; v. 4)
Includes bibliographical references and index.
1. Internet and women. 2. Internet—Social aspects.
3. Technology and women. 4. Sex in popular culture. I. Title.
HQ1178.S46   303.48'33082—dc22   2008022589
ISBN 978-0-8204-5694-2
ISSN 1526-3169

Bibliographic information published by **Die Deutsche Bibliothek**.
Die Deutsche Bibliothek lists this publication in the "Deutsche
Nationalbibliografie"; detailed bibliographic data is available
on the Internet at http://dnb.ddb.de/.

Cover design by Irene J. Silva

© 2008 Peter Lang Publishing, Inc., New York
29 Broadway, 18th floor, New York, NY 10006
www.peterlang.com

Printed in the United States of America

CAMGIRLS

Digital Formations

Steve Jones
General Editor

Vol. 4

PETER LANG
New York • Washington, D.C./Baltimore • Bern
Frankfurt am Main • Berlin • Brussels • Vienna • Oxford

For the first and most influential feminist in my life

Veronica Elizabeth Senft.

Table of Contents

Acknowledgments

I am profoundly grateful to all the camgirls and viewers who helped me understand their world, especially Ana Voog, Melissa Gira, ArtVamp, Ducky Doolittle, Lisa Batey, Vera Little, Andrea Mignolo, Cera Byer, Jennifer Ringley, Stacy Pershall, Amanda, Flare, and Lux. Although I thank everyone on my LiveJournal "Friends List" for their support, I am especially indebted to Laura Fokkena, Helena Kvarnestrom, John Styn, Alan MacIntyre, Scott Ecksel, Mia Lipner, Auriea Harvey, Melissa DiMauro, Eric Durchholz, Cathy Mancuso, and Julie Levin Russo for their insights. On Echo, Morgan Noel, Greg Sewell, Clive Thompson, Maura Johnston, Emily Nussbaum, Jack Taylor, Max Whitney, Andrew Hearst, Paul Wallich, Joe Hobaica, and the Wack Group read portions of this manuscript at key times, and I remain grateful for their feedback.

In my offline world, I want to thank my former advisor Barbara Kirshenblatt-Gimblett for her unflagging support, my editors Damon Zucca and Mary Savigar for encouragement at precisely the right moments, my 'discourse partner' Jodi Dean for her invaluable contributions to my thinking, Jennifer Fink for her ability to cut to the heart of any intellectual project, and Steve Jones, who continues to serve as a shining example of how to do media studies the right way. I am particularly indebted to my friend danah boyd, a true pioneer in the field of social network research, who encouraged me to submit a copy of this manuscript to her colleagues in a digital reading group at the Annenberg School. To say their critiques and comments influenced the final manuscript is understatement *in extremis*.

I changed jobs a number of times during the writing of this book and at each, I was fortunate enough to have enthusiastic co-workers willing to listen to my ideas at length. I owe Niki Parisier, Patrick McCreery, and Vanessa Manko at NYU's Gallatin School for their patience, NYU's Interactive Telecommunications Program for its expertise and equipment, and all my students for their brilliance. I was introduced to online ethnography by Annette Markham, and was fortunate enough to work with her at the University of the Virgin Islands, where she helped shape this book's political agenda. I finished this project while at the University of East London, U.K., and want to thank Marta Rabikowska, Paul Gormley, and Jonathan Hardy for their enthusiasm as I reached the end of my writing.

Finally, this project would have never come to fruition if not for five individuals. My brothers Michael and T.J.—who are always there when I need them—provided me with a new computer just as my own one died (and it is hard to be a camgirl without a computer.) My friend Tom Igoe not only happily suffered my ruminations, he also set up a webcam for his cat Noodles in New York, which makes my days in London much happier. Of the people who have supported me intellectually over the years, I perhaps owe Angus Johnston the greatest debt, for teaching me that the only way to hit a moving target is to think about today as a historian does. My last thanks goes to my best friend Kim Scheinberg, who doesn't have the word 'impossible' in her vocabulary.

Introduction: The Personal as Political in the Age of the Global Network

In late 1999, I set up a webcam in my bedroom. I had told my friend Jennifer Fink that I was writing about camgirls—women who broadcast themselves over the Web for the general public, while trying to cultivate a measure of celebrity in the process—and she suggested I ought to run a "homecam" of my own for a while. At the very least, she reasoned, the gesture would allow me to introduce myself to my subjects as someone sympathetically allied with their subculture, rather than as an outsider merely interested in writing a book.

I still have flashbacks of that first day homecamming. I spent an hour adjusting and readjusting my hair, makeup, and lighting, feeling nauseated just thinking about my vanity, and fretting over the folly of broadcasting my image to anyone with a computer and an interest in watching. I was also squeamish about the political implications of such an act: Was this really the future of women in new media? Over the following eighteen months, my nausea would be replaced by wonder, challenge, and a sense of community until finally, restless for something new, I shut the camera down.

This book is an ethnographic and critical study of one generation of camgirls and their viewers from 2000 to 2004. Its narrative follows that of the camgirl phenomenon itself, beginning with the earliest experiments in personal homecamming and ending with the newest forms of identity and community being articulated through social networking sites like LiveJournal, YouTube, MySpace and Facebook.[1] It is grounded in interviews, performance analysis of events transpiring between camgirls and their viewers, and my own experiences as an ersatz camgirl.[2]

Had you visited my unoriginally-titled Terricam site during its heyday, you would have seen a close-up image of my face and neck set against a rust background, along with the following text:

Welcome to, uh, me. Click here for a popup view of the cam that will refresh every thirty seconds, unless my system crashes. Then I have to drink some iced coffee, stress out and put things right. I am on a 56 K modem, so the tech isn't pretty. Because my resources are scant, this isn't a 24/7 webcam. I do my best, but sometimes my best doesn't cut it. I should also warn you that I've been WICKED busy teaching and writing this semester. God only knows when I'll be in chat, etc. In the meantime, why not do some reading?[3]

The site contained a link to my homepage, as well as links to my academic and personal papers. For those interested in my daily musings, I provided a pointer to my page on LiveJournal, the blogging site of choice among camgirls.[4] There was also a chat room (which broke every few days), and information on how to contact me via instant message or email. These extras were intended to compensate for the fact that all my viewers ever really got to see was a grainy image of me at my computer, me reading on my bed, or me putting my coat on.

In the Beginning

The viewers who chose to follow the links soon discovered my preoccupation with my deceased mother. In the latter part of the 1960's, she joined thousands of other women who (to use the jargon of the time) found their minds blown by books like Betty Friedan's *Feminine Mystique*. During this time, my mother was slowly beginning to suspect that certain problems that she had long thought of as personal—comments made to her on the street, moments when her views were dismissed as unimportant, times when she couldn't get my father to share in child-rearing responsibilities—might be part of a larger social condition.

Figure 1. Scenes from the Terricam.

By the 1970's, my mother was attending meetings at the Junior Women's Club, the closest thing to a 'consciousness-raising' group in our town. "A consciousness-raising group consists of a small number of women (generally not more than twelve) who meet informally once a week at a member's home or women's center," reads a pamphlet of the time. "Ask friends to bring friends—it isn't necessary to know everyone. Sisterhood is a warm feeling!"[5]

My mother was beginning to discover that the personal is political. While the origin of that phrase remains a subject of some debate, most feminist historians credit Carol Hanisch's 1970 essay of the same name.[6] It was written in response to male activists who saw consciousness-raising as 'therapy' rather than a legitimate form of politics. "One of the first things we discover[ed] in these groups is that personal problems are political problems," Hanisch wrote thirty years later. "There is only collective action for a collective solution ..."[7]

Eventually I would be exposed to a consciousness-raising of my own generation. In the early 1990's, many young American women found themselves frustrated by the narrowness of the roles available to them in the burgeoning independent (indie) music scene.[8] Men culturally dominated indie music bands, magazines, and fashion just as they physically dominated the scene's mosh pits. Riot Grrl was a personal-as-political response to this marginalization, and in the same way that consciousness-raising groups had encouraged women to 'bring a friend' a generation earlier, the 'Riot Grrl' movement urged women to mail xeroxed copies of homemade "zines" (short for magazines) on indie and do-it-yourself culture to anyone willing to provide the postage.[9] Soon, those zines began to migrate to the Web in the form of personal homepages.

Today—more than fifteen years after Riot Grrl—the rise of webcams, blogs and media-generated 'confession culture' presents a real challenge to those who believe that sharing personal experience is still a political act. Now one concern is that women's mediated sharing of life experiences—whether through memoir, 'reality' genres, or even auto-ethnographies—is less likely to alienate men than to titillate them. Sisterhood may still induce a 'warm feeling,' but for some of us, it's the wrong sort of warm.

For other women, the danger is not so much titillation as a paralyzing solipsism that isolates rather than connects those who can help us recognize the personal as political. Feminist scholar Rita Felski, for one, is skeptical:

> Is the act of confessing a liberating step for women, which uncovers the political dimensions of the personal experience, confronts the contradictions of existing gender roles, and creates an important sense of female identification and solidarity? Or does this kind of [confession] uncritically reiterate the "jargon of authenticity" and ideology of subjectivity-as-truth which feminism should be calling into question?[10]

The Work of the Web in the Age of Digital Reproduction

Here is an experiment: set up a webcam and announce to everyone in the room that it is broadcasting to the Web. Now point it toward someone, and see how long that person holds out before checking their image; I think the longest anyone has ever gone in my home is about five minutes. I suppose I shouldn't have been surprised when I discovered that the Canadian television crew who'd been sent down to interview me were hamming it up for my webcam. The crew even started reading my journal once they realized my readers were commenting on what they saw. "My striped shirt is a big hit in Japan!" the cameraman joked after someone from Tokyo posted to that effect. "Tell them the shirt's from Germany," he added. I had thought people working in the television industry would be beyond such things. I was wrong.

"Every day the urge grows stronger to get hold of an object at very close range by way of its likeness, its reproduction," wrote Walter Benjamin in a famous 1936 essay.[11] In the mechanical age, the introduction of photography and cinema led to an aesthetic that art critic Robert Hughes dubbed 'the shock of the new.'[12] Mass access to these technologies of reproduction had the effect of successfully shattering once and for all what Benjamin called 'aura': our near-religious worship of authenticity in art. For Benjamin, the destruction of aura was a positive thing—if everything might be a duplicate, a democratization of art-making was at hand.

In the digital age, the shock of the new takes a slightly different form. If mechanics introduced people to the pleasure of transforming authenticity through reproduction, digital technologies afford us the opportunity to produce and distribute *ourselves* as copies. In the mechanical age, the man wearing a striped shirt in New York marvels that someone in Japan is commenting on his clothing. In the digital age, he engages with the person viewing him at a distance, annotating his self-presentation in order to allow himself to be more fully known.

There are those who would argue that a 'confession' regarding the origin of one's shirt is hardly a political act—unless perhaps a conversation on clothing production and globalization follows. But on the Web, just as in the consciousness-raising groups of the 1970's, the fact of communication itself has political import, even where the content of the communication appears not to. When we want to know what something 'means' on the Web, it's useful to remember Marshall McLuhan's injunction that the medium is the message. On the Web, the medium of exchange is not dialogue, but rather dialectic.

Web dialectic begins when we present our images, gestures and words for consumption by various audiences. In response, those audiences produce portraits, stories, counter-points, and even satires of their own. We are then faced with a choice: either we respond to their responses, or we do not.

When we do (hoping to correct, alter, or extend their interpretations of us), the status of our self-representation shifts. Rather than performing as passive objects for the consumption of others, we demand recognition as living subjects. Our demand to be recognized as a subject takes the form of words, images, and gestures that will in turn be circulated as representational objects among audiences, and the cycle continues.

A perfect example of the dialectical nature of Web exchange can be found in the genesis of this book. In the course of my research, I corresponded with approximately forty camgirls and nearly eighty homecam viewers, and conducted formal interviews with ten camgirls and twenty-one viewers. Ultimately, I was able to speak face-to-face with fifteen of those thirty-one formal subjects. We met in various places: in their homes, at conferences, and during events such as LiveJournal gatherings.[13] Every person interviewed for this book was contacted in advance of publication, and nearly all of my subjects asked to kept informed about my research as it progressed. To facilitate that process, I periodically posted draft chapters on LiveJournal. There, my 500 'friends' could correct, amplify, or simply comment on what I'd written. Often their comments would provoke multi-sided conversations that gave me new insight into the issues I was exploring. I've quoted portions of those conversations throughout this book.

My point bears repeating: on the Web, the dialectical nature of communication is itself political in nature, *regardless of content*, particularly if one understands politics as the leveraging of power between connected entities. Viewed in this light, the contemporary denigration of (implicitly feminine) 'personal' journals by the readers and writers of (implicitly masculine) political blogs recapitulates the dismissal of consciousness-raising groups by 'real' political activists a generation ago.

The Challenge of Network Society

Thus far, I have argued that the dialectical nature of Web exchange can serve those who wish to make the personal political in the time of network society, even as it presents far greater risks than older forms of networking such as consciousness-raising. Now, I want to consider the challenges network society *itself* poses for feminists.

Human beings have always been enmeshed in complex social network structures such as food webs, semantic webs, and economic webs. Yet according to Manuel Castells, 'networked society' differs from these ancient modes of organization in that today we rely on our computers to process and manage the information necessary for us to live with ourselves, and one another.[14]

As an example, consider the global economy: Because of linked computer systems, the global economy now processes "billions of dollars in mere seconds," notes Castells, adding, "And that can change from values to values, from markets to markets, from currencies to currencies, which increases the complexity, the size, and, ultimately, the volatility of global financial markets around the world." Castells argues that the upshot of the global economy is that it "makes extremely difficult any kind of monetary and budget policy which does not take into consideration the global financial market."[15]

For feminists, network society presents a double-edged sword. On the one hand, it permits women around the world to use technologies of travel and information as never before, enabling them to escape their cities and countries of origin, work remotely, and distribute media over the Internet. For some women the changes have been nothing short of miraculous. In his examination of international survey data, Castells notes how global networks have enabled "a mass insurrection of women against their oppression throughout the world, albeit with different intensity depending on culture and country."[16] Jodi Dean lists some examples of this insurrection: fewer women marrying; more children born to single parent households; women as an increasing percentage of the paid global workforce.[17]

Yet it is not quite time to start celebrating post-patriarchy. Women and girls still constitute seventy percent of the world's poor, do two-thirds of the world's work, earn less than one-tenth of its income, and own less than one-hundredth of its property.[18] For those who do work, networks create "intense exploitation of labor, especially female labor."[19] Although Third World sweatshop workers and outsourced call center laborers are the most frequently publicized examples of this exploitation, equally significant and too often ignored are those who migrate to the First World to work in unregulated fields such as house cleaning, child rearing, elder care, and sex work.[20]

"If this is post-patriarchy," writes Jodi Dean, "something is missing."[21] The "something missing" is the economic equity and access to democracy promised by proponents of network society. Unfortunately, the belief that everyone counts in network society—or will, once they are given access—is a naïve one. As Andrew Calcutt points out, technology use alone is a poor indicator of social power: "the CEO who has not got time to send emails and values his privacy so much he refuses to carry a mobile phone, would be counted among the 'information-poor:' while the woman working in a call center for little more than the minimum wage, appears in the list of 'information-rich.'"[22] Yet until this personal data is used as a tool for political action, notes Dean, we will continue to live in a culture that believes "anyone can be discovered, that everyone is unique, that everyone counts, everyone has a voice, that on the Web everyone has a home page."[23]

The critiques made above are particularly relevant to camgirls—at least to the ones I studied. As a group, these camgirls were a more or less homogenous lot in terms of race, class, and chosen language. Nearly all hailed from wealthier, high-teledensity areas such as North America, Europe, the Southern Cone region of South America, and Australia.[24] Although some, such as Argentina's Anabella of Anabella.com, made a point of writing in their native language, most homecam sites are in English.[25] Most camgirls I studied were white, able-bodied, straight or bisexual, and less than forty years old.[26] Perhaps most tellingly, I have yet to come across a camgirl who doesn't have access to a private room for broadcasting. This last factor may help explain why I had particular trouble locating women in places such as the Middle East (excepting Israel) and Africa (excepting South Africa), as these regions tend to have public telecenters rather than private Internet connections.

Space, Time, and the Presentations of Self

Women who wish to engage the personal as political in an age of networks need to understand that networked communication tends to complicate earlier ideas regarding appropriate ways to organize. Early consciousness-raising groups were often contentious and sometimes fractious. The women in them might differ intensely in life experience, or in their views on sexuality, work, motherhood, or any number of other questions. But they had more-or-less clear boundaries in space and time—each meeting had a beginning and an end, and each was conducted in a private space among participants who were known to one another. The communities examined in this book confound traditional conceptions of public and private, open and closed, creating profound implications for their participants.

One concept developed at length throughout this book is that of friendship. For women in consciousness-raising, 'bringing a friend' meant finding a like-minded woman from one's social circle and inviting her to a meeting. While live events were important to Riot Grrls, the rise of 'zine culture allowed women to build additional networks beyond their face-to-face contacts. Today, on social networking spaces like LiveJournal, MySpace and Facebook, 'bringing a friend' amounts to clicking a button, and one's words and images have as good a chance of landing in front of hostile eyes as friendly ones.

These new developments force us to make difficult decisions regarding our 'presentation of self' according to perceived audience, a largely intuitive process in the offline world. Offline, the self I might present to a Riot Grrl group is not the one I present to my brothers, and the one I present to a lover is not the one I present to a colleague—or a different lover. There is sometimes overlap among these audiences, but that overlap (or, as warranted, distinction) is itself managed and facilitated by physical boundaries: I can change my self presentation as I move from the bedroom to the classroom, and from the classroom to the bar.

Although it is possible to compartmentalize online, it's not easy—just ask anyone on Facebook who has agonized over blocking a 'friends' request. Online, our public persona is utterly integrated—we can present different selves to different audiences in private email, but each of these selves must somehow be consistent with the self we create for our LiveJournal, or our homepage, or our webcam, unless we decide to develop entirely new personae and accounts for each of our new 'selves.'

Offline, we are protected from ourselves by the passage of time. Even when others recall our most embarrassing moments, they are filtered through the gauze of memory. Online, the words and images with which we associate ourselves persist indefinitely, retaining their exact original form long after the context of their creation has been lost and the self who created them has been discarded. Most of us who started online in the 1980's or 1990's can readily summon up a list of cringe-worthy documents of our past selves, long deleted but still locatable through search engines like the Wayback Machine.[27]

Finally, anyone who enters into networked space is confronted with the dilemma of how and whether to trust an incompletely known other. An executive asked to divulge her banking details to a tele-worker may appear to have little in common with a woman who strips for public viewing on her webcam, but both routinely provide intimate details about their lives to people whom they may never meet face to face, people with whom they would otherwise never be connected.

Publicity, Branding and Emotional Labor

I have spoken above about some of the dilemmas of the networked age—confession, trust, compartmentalization. I've talked about camgirls' relevance to some of these questions, and will explore them all in more detail in the pages that follow. But it is also important to understand how the camgirls I studied served as 'beta testers' for a range of techniques that have been taken up at a global level on video sharing sites like YouTube, and social networking sites like MySpace and Facebook. Three of these techniques discussed at length in this book are the generation of celebrity, building of self as brand, and engagement in a specific form of emotional labor.

I became aware of the power of celebrity early on in my homecamming tenure. I was not the first academic to have a webcam—Sandy Stone's now-defunct SandyCam began broadcasting from her office back in 1999.[28] To my knowledge, however, I was the first academic camgirl, garnering a tiny measure of 'fame' for my efforts. My small but somewhat enthusiastic fan base began to grow after links to the Terricam appeared briefly on the sites of Jennifer Ringley and Ana Voog, two icons of the homecamming movement.[29] These endorsements, and press coverage I received later, brought an influx of strangers into my life for which I was utterly unprepared. I went from occasionally going into my chat room to goof off with friends, to arriving and seeing ten or fifteen unfamiliar names.

> "Hi," I would type. "Who are you folks?"
> "We followed the link to your site from Slate.com," they would respond.
> "Oh. Great! Um, how's it going?" I would ask.
> "Good. You're on Slate.com today," they would repeat.

Eventually I realized that these people felt they were owed some entertainment. After all, someone pointed out, I had gotten some publicity by branding myself as the "camgirl writing about camgirls."[30] And with press coverage comes the obligation to be press-worthy. Was I supposed to put on a show? Ask them about their lives? Talk about my work? What exactly did I think my product was? And what were my 'consumers' expecting to consume?

The camgirl's self-presentation as a brand in an attention economy is particularly interesting in light of what sociologist Arlie Hochschild calls 'emotional labor.' In her 1984 book *The Managed Heart,* Hochschild studied flight attendants, bill collectors and other workers with jobs that required them to induce particular emotional states in others.[31] She theorized that for emotional laborers, work functions dramaturgically, with the worker as actor, the customers as audience, and the work environment as a stage.

To manage their emotional states, employees engage in two sorts of acting. 'Surface acting' is the equivalent of faking a smile or acting as a character without personally identifying with the role one is playing. In 'deep acting,' the employee works to identify with the feelings she needs to project to keep customers satisfied. Whether she engages in the acting consciously or unconsciously, and whether she enjoys herself or not, this acting requires effort, which Hochschild qualifies as labor, arguing, "When deep gestures of exchange enter the market sector and are bought and sold as an aspect of labor power, feelings are commoditized."[32]

Are You a Feminist?

Because this book is an explicitly feminist one, I feel honor-bound to point out that most of my subjects expressed ambivalence about feminism. "I hear that word used by many people in so many ways," camgirl Jennifer Ringley told me, "I prefer not to call myself anything at all."[33] Webcam viewer Amy observed likewise that although she "admires a lot of feminists," she does not claim the word for herself. "I think of myself as a free woman," Amy explained, "and in some ways I am significantly more free than men."[34] After a series of fascinating exchanges about women, agency, and new media, camgirl viewer Alan wrote me that he had "excuses, good ones," why he didn't want to be called a feminist.[35] When I expressed confusion, Alan explained that he couldn't identify as feminist because "popular culture screams at me, constantly." Like many men I interviewed, Alan felt that feminism required him to assume personal blame for all the effects of patriarchy—something he didn't feel emotionally equipped to do.

Some women and men I spoke with did identity as feminist, defining the term in varying ways. "If it means believing in the equality of the sexes," wrote viewer Frank, known online as Grass, "yes I am."[36] Webcam viewer Scott Ecksel told me that, "although there has been real progress, our society remains extremely sexist; women have been shafted for millennia, and I want to work towards correcting that disgrace."[37] Others identified as feminist with reservations. Andrea Mignolo, formerly of the cam-house HereandNow, said an international perspective has always influenced her thinking on feminism:

> My father is a postcolonial theorist of sorts, and as I grew more interested in feminist theory in college, he would talk with me about what I was learning. He drew my focus to the women in other parts of the world who don't agree with the thoughts and pressure that traditional Western feminists place on third-world women.[38]

She associates the term first and foremost with Western feminism, so for Andrea 'feminist' is as loaded a term as 'camgirl.' "I don't say that I am either," she writes, "but many people have called me both." Melissa Gira, a student majoring in ancient religions at the University of Massachusetts, agrees. "I am a feminist in part," She says, "but I have to do a fair amount of bolstering my politics with sex radical feminism."[39] For Melissa, a useable feminism is one that can take seriously the "power of sexual transgression and marginality."

Not So 1998

Unsurprisingly, things have changed a great deal since I began this project—at least technologically. Just a few years ago, it took a significant level of comfort with the Internet to configure a webcam. Now many computers are video-enabled by default—there are even services to help users *disable* the camera built into every MacBook. P. David Marshall reminds us that in the first stage of a technology, machines themselves feature as the star of their own show.[40] During the early days of television, cameras rolled while orchestras played. In the earliest days of webcams, people were happy to watch corn grow. And just as some people continue to visit the Corn Cam, some camgirls still have diehard viewers willing to watch their silent cameras refresh at thirty-second intervals.[41] For the most part, however, their time has passed. As a nineteen-year-old at the South by Southwest (SXSW) New Media Conference in 2001 wearily explained to me, "Camgirls are so 1998."[42]

Of all my original research subjects, only two (Ana Voog of AnaCam and Anabella of AnabellaCam) still homecam full time. Lisa Batey has now resumed broadcasting on the streaming site Justin.tv after a long hiatus.[43] My other camgirl subjects have either stopped homecamming entirely, or continue their sites only sporadically. This progression appears to be typical of many camgirls between 1998 and 2003. With the exception of Ana Voog, most camgirls with whom I began my research think of webcamming today less as a lifelong commitment, and more as a creative phase that they entered deeply into for a time, became overexposed to, and then abandoned, to pick it up later as something to be engaged in only when the mood strikes.

Some women still aspire to camgirl fame today, but those women and their viewers inhabit a different subcultural "scene" than the ones in this book. Perhaps the most obvious difference is that the women I focused on were in their mid-twenties and thirties, whereas the next generation of camgirls are primarily in their late teens and early twenties. Although I briefly touch upon latter-day camgirl cultures in what follows, they are ultimately outside the scope of my research. The next generation of camgirls deserve their own book, but this isn't it.

There are at least three reasons for the fading of the camgirl phenomenon as it existed at the end of the 20th century. The first, discussed above, was the cultural saturation of webcams beyond early adopters. The second has to do with the rapid rise of broadband penetration around the world. The third was the rise of social networking services that now easily support text, still images, audio and video. Among camgirls, the blogging service of choice still remains LiveJournal, which prior to the advent of MySpace and Facebook was the "largest structured networked community online," hosting approximately 13 million journals.[44] Even when they abandon their webcams, camgirls still continue to keep their social networks alive, a fact which will become obvious toward the end of this book.

Given the rapid spread and adoption of the technologies discussed above, the issues which were "so 1998" for camgirl communities are now "so 2008" for the rest of us. Network theory—once of interest only to some social and computer scientists—is quickly going mainstream. Dutch political theorists Maarten Hajer and Hendrik Wagenaar have detailed what they see as the major political challenges of our network age: a rise in charismatic symbols, a state of radical uncertainty about the future, a demand for translation of difference, and a desire for new ways to generate trust.[45] In the chapters that follow, I use camgirl communities as case studies to explore these and other challenges.

The End of the Beginning

I raise a lot of topics in this book that I would have liked to have addressed in more detail, and there were many moments when I had to set a subject aside to keep from further burdening an already overstuffed project. As a result, many of the ideas I express in these pages are still in the early stages of development. I am excited by the work that others are doing in these areas, and am eager to engage with and learn from their perspectives as I continue to articulate my own.

When I started this book, people would look at me strangely when I said I was going to lay the emotional labor of camgirls side by side with that of nannies. I think I've made a strong case in this book that they're worth thinking about together, but the subject is one on which I see tremendous potential for further research. Laura Augustin's work on domestic laborers, Gavin Poynter's on teleworkers and Heather Montgomery's on child sex workers are models of the kind of scholarship I find exemplary, and I look forward to seeing what is revealed by future ethnographies of other categories of emotional laborers.[46]

Teen sexual expression over the internet is a subject that doesn't just deserve its own book, it deserves its own series. Teenagers, and children, own these technologies. My seven-year-old nephew has an email account. We live in a mediated culture; should it continue to surprise us that our children are expressing themselves through media? We must also face the fact that for many young girls today, sexual expression and self-expression are of a piece—even chastity bracelets are a form of self-expression via sexual expression. I don't want to say that ethnography is a cure-all, but it seems to me that the best way to initiate dialogue with any group about their behavior is to ask them what it is they think they're doing, and then listen when they respond.

I'm also deeply interested in the human face of what I call networked reflective solidarity. It's now possible to go to kiva.org and give money to someone who's engaging in a microfinance project half a world away.[47] I want to know whether the interpersonal communication that results from such donations is doomed to be a stilted and synthetic replica of 'charity correspondence' of the past, or if something more dynamic, more human, can be exchanged. The technology exists, but do we have the capacity to give people a hearing as well as giving them our money, and are we willing to change our voices as we encounter theirs?

In the process of writing this book, there were several moments when I became so inspired by a topic that my research and writing took on a life of its own. This impulse, and my willingness to give it rein, has led me to conceptualize two additional books, one on micro-celebrity and one on tele-ethicality, which are consuming ever more of my attention as the work on this book draws to a close.

Micro-celebrity initially seemed like it was going to be a fun and easy topic, but it has led me to places that I didn't intend to go, and I find that it speaks to our moment in unexpected ways. Conversely, I initially conceived the tele-ethicality project as a dry one, but no topic I have taken on has ever sparked so much lively discussion among friends and strangers. I think this is because ethics doesn't begin with dictates—it begins with stories. When you and I share a story, there are multiple positions for us to inhabit, multiple scenarios to explore, and multiple outcomes to contemplate. As Gayatri Spivak reminds us, ethics calls us to stay long enough to listen to what others have to say, especially when what they are saying strikes us as irrational, backward, or at odds with what we perceive to be their interests—or ours.[48]

Throughout the writing of this book, I have been engaged in a dialogue with friends, colleagues, subjects, and other readers. That dialogue continues, and it is my hope that the book's publication will invigorate it. I will be writing and speaking on the subjects I have raised here in a variety of venues in the months and years to come, and I invite you to join in the conversation at www.terrisenft.net.

1. Keeping it Real on the Web: Authenticity, Celebrity, Branding

"OMG. Did you know that Jenny shut her cam down?"

This was how my new year began in 2004, with five emails from strangers wanting me to help them understand why the Web's first and most famous camgirl had turned off her cameras and closed down her site.[1]

The JenniCam had gone live in 1996, broadcasting from Jennifer Ringley's Dickinson College dorm room. Its audience consisted of anyone with Web access and an interest in watching, and its numbers increased dramatically the first time Ringley transmitted live footage of sex with her then-boyfriend. When Ringley wasn't home, viewers were invited to look at her photo archives, read her diaries, talk to one another on her bulletin board, or to visit the Web pages of her friends. By the time it closed, the JenniCam had established itself as the best known of all personal webcam sites, registering 100 million hits per week at its peak in 1998.[2]

Some of us had seen the shutdown coming. Jennifer had been saying for weeks that her new job was taking her away from the camera for hours at a time, and had been expressing frustration with PayPal's recent decision to block transactions for sites offering 'adult' content. But the closing of JenniCam still marked the end of an era in which a camgirl could become a celebrity of sorts, embodying "fame after photography," as the Museum of Modern Art had dubbed it.[3]

Jennifer Ringley was not the Web's first star. Five years before the JenniCam went live, computer scientist Quentin Stafford-Fraser had a resource problem. Fifteen staffers at Cambridge University shared a small-capacity, first-come-first-served coffeepot, and those close enough to smell the fresh-brewed coffee had an advantage over those on other floors. In an attempt to level the playing field, Stafford-Fraser pointed a small camera at the coffee machine and sent the images to the staff's computer network for remote viewing. Later, the Trojan Room Coffee Cam went on the Web, garnering a total of more than 2 million hits before it went offline in 2001.[4]

The JenniCam's historical antecedents stretch back even further, to a 19th century genre of reality-as-entertainment: the Victorian sensation drama. These plays were essentially demonstrations of technology, in which waterfalls, locomotives, and court cases were simulated on stage to 'thrill and chill' audiences with displays of 'theatrical authenticity'—verisimilitude delivered by the representational mechanisms of the era (chiefly the microphone, the phonograph and the film projector). Though some have characterized the audiences for these spectacles as credulous, theater historian Lynn Voskuil argues that sensation playgoers were England's first truly consumerist audiences, simultaneously enjoying and critiquing the 'so real' phenomena placed on stage for their entertainment.[5] Like sensation drama audiences, homecam viewers enjoy the images, sounds, and textual interactions transpiring on their screens while simultaneously engaging in sustained critiques of the "so real" that put most reporters and academics to shame.

Reality, Realism, and The Real

In an interview she gave at the height of her popularity, Jennifer Ringley told ABC News that she wanted to "show people that what we see on TV—people with perfect hair, perfect friends, perfect lives—is not reality. I'm reality."[6] This was an audacious claim, and given the ubiquity of terms like 'reality,' 'realism,' 'reality entertainment,' and even 'hyperreal' in popular and scholarly writing on camgirls, it strikes me as one worth discussing.[7]

To make sense of Ringley's contention, we must first establish a frame of reference: Clearly, her webcam was 'real' in some ways that, say, a situation comedy is not, since sitcoms are explicitly fictional. The JenniCam was also real in ways that 'reality entertainment' productions tend not to be. A reality television show uses non-actors as performers, but it often places them in contrived circumstances. At least as important, reality television is almost always heavily edited, with the editing process shaping the narrative powerfully. By contrast, homecamming takes place in 'real' time—live and without overt manipulation.

And yet, though Jennifer Ringley is certainly, as she says, "real," her webcam's relationship to reality remains equivocal. Her claim that she is more "real" than television personalities with "perfect hair, perfect friends and perfect lives" also raises the related question of representation—it should be remembered that at the time that Ringley was broadcasting, she was a tall, blonde, conventionally attractive woman in her twenties.

Figure 2. Camgirl aesthetics 101. At the JenniCam site, a small live image (to the right of the "start here" command) gave viewers a taste of what the site offers. "Chat now" led to a public bulletin board, inhabited mostly by long-time JenniCam fans, rather than Jennifer herself. Courtesy Jennifer Ringley.

Figure 3. Camgirl aesthetics 102. Amanda's face was always visible at the Amandacam site, but the "guest cam" link had to be chosen in order to view her live webcam. Amanda routinely chatted with her viewers in her "members" section, which also provides viewers access to nine webcams. "Oliver" refers to Amanda's dog, and "47 covers" are magazine-style headshots of Amanda. Courtesy Amanda.

Figure 4. Camgirl aesthetics 103. Ana Voog of AnaCam leaves her live image large on the site's menu page. In the top left-hand corner, she's activated a random word-generating program. Clicking on each of the images on the right leads to journals, bulletin boards, fan art pages, and Ana's artwork and crochet projects. There are links to RAINN (Rape Abuse and Incest National Network), RAWA (Revolutionary Association of the Women of Afghanistan), and SHP (Street Harassment Project.) Courtesy Ana Voog.

Going Backstage: Technical Requirements

The theatrical authenticity of the camgirl begins with the webcam. Given the range of uses to which webcams are routinely put today, it is important to distinguish homecamming (the technique camgirls employ) from other practices. As the term suggests, homecamming is conducted from the domestic sphere, and camgirls tend to have at least one camera in the bedroom, although they almost never place one in the bathroom. Most audiences quickly discover that they will most often find a camgirl broadcasting from the same place we all use computers: at a table, in some home office setup.

Every webcam image is (like those created by any digital camera) made up of tiny dots of color—pixels. The more pixels, the clearer the image. Most webcams today advertise a resolution of 640 × 480 pixels. In their ongoing quest for higher pixel rates and greater visual clarity, many camgirls eschew off-the-shelf webcams for higher-end video cameras modified with capture devices set to grab shots at predetermined intervals.

Jennifer Ringley's house was equipped with nine cameras, but delivered only one silent, still image, once every five minutes. Most camgirls today opt for much more frequent shots than this, and some camgirls feature streaming audio and video in their broadcasts. Because a webcam presents a series of still pictures rather than a moving image, the narrative it offers is necessarily ambiguous and incomplete. A webcam, particularly one with a slow refresh rate, engages the viewer in the process of constructing the story she is watching unfold. Here is one of Ana's favorite examples of the disjuncture between image, action, and intent that occurs on her webcams each day:

> Okay, I am sitting on my couch, in tears. I have a horrible migraine, and the pain is getting worse. My boyfriend Jason comes into the apartment and asks me what is wrong. I tell him about my headache and he goes to the pharmacy to get medicine for me. I sit on the couch, crying, with my stereo playing in the background (I am always playing music, and most times I've had "streaming sound" on my cam, I just use the audio as a radio station, playing my favorite music to my silent images). Ten minutes later, I check my email, and there are twenty messages telling me how horrible my boyfriend is to make me cry and then walk out on me, and how they'd never treat me that way. This is why I say over and over, my cams aren't about me—they are about YOU. What are you feeling today, that you saw that series of images and made those connections?[8]

Whatever format they choose, camgirls must compress their broadcasts before they are released online. Compression reduces file size at a small cost in image quality. Once compressed, the material is sent via modem to an Internet service provider (ISP), and directed to an address on the Web for public viewing, live and unedited. In addition, nearly all camgirl sites contain archives of older shots for audience perusal. Because it would take an unreasonable amount of storage space to house all the images taken of a camgirl every day, and because editing the archives allows a camgirl to manage her self-presentation, these archives are always culled substantially.

When the JenniCam appeared, the Web was in its infancy. Ringley was justly proud of the fact that she hand-coded the HTML on her site, since consumer-friendly home page authoring software such as FrontPage or DreamWeaver were unavailable to the general public. Today, people don't even need to know how to use authoring programs to establish a personal home page. Within minutes, users traveling to sites like MySpace or LiveJournal can set up their sites, choose appropriate theme music and even embed videos, all with a few clicks.

Finances

In 2000, homecamming was an expensive endeavor. For starters, the most basic low-resolution webcam cost upward of $100, and in countries without an established consumer electronics industry, the costs took on a new dimension. "A Logitech webcam costs you US$100," Anabella of Argentina's AnabellaCam explained to me in 2001, "but a dealer importing that cam to sell here would have to price it at least US$150, which is more than a month's pay for most people here."⁹Although lower-speed modems were still available, many camgirls in the U.S. opted for DSL or broadband connectivity, costing between US$30–60 per month.

A camgirl's equipment and Internet access costs were more or less fixed in those days, but the cost of broadcasting was variable and unpredictable. It was common then to hear camgirls speak at length about the price of bandwidth: the fees charged by ISPs for transmission of information to end users. Today most users' bandwidth might as well be unmetered—a parent can sit in a public park and broadcast images of her child's new skateboarding technique live to her in-laws without ever giving thought to who is paying for that service. In 2000, however, ISPs would typically 'serve' only a few megabytes of data before charging additional fees. A moderately popular site could easily rack up charges in the hundreds of dollars.

And as a camgirl's traffic rose higher her costs ballooned, as Jennifer Ringley learned not long after she started the JenniCam in 1996. In the online diary she maintained at her Web site, many of her entries expressed concerns about money. According to Ringley, the JenniCam (which, as noted earlier, displayed only still, silent images with a slow refresh rate) racked up bills in excess of US$15,000 per month.[10]

To defray these costs, some camgirls chose to segregate their sites into free and subscription-based 'members only' sections, charging viewers US$5 or more per month for access to additional features. In Jennifer's case, the only difference between the two was that the camera's refresh rate was higher in the for-pay area. Amanda of the now-defunct AmandaCam gave paid viewers access to additional cameras in her house beyond those seen by free viewers.[11] Ana Voog of AnaCam runs a private bulletin board and adds artistic 'special features' on her for-pay site.

When homecamming was in its heyday, it was common for journalists and viewers to suggest that top camgirls were earning extravagant incomes from subscription fees, but such speculation is hard to credit. Jennifer Ringley long maintained that she never made money off her webcam—at the height of her popularity (when she would have been taking in the most subscription fees), Jennifer was also at the height of her bandwidth costs. Once, Amanda of AmandaCam intimated to me that she made a respectable income running her webcam. Because she was part of the homecamming boom, I am tempted to believer her. Yet each time I pressed Amanda for information about her profits, she deflected my questions by speaking about her labor, mentioning how she made a point of chatting every day with subscribers so that they came to feel like they were part of a 'family'.

While the possibility perhaps existed to make money from homecamming a few years ago, today fewer viewers and more free content elsewhere on the web means far less money from subscribers. Ana Voog, probably the most popular camgirl broadcasting in 2008, only makes a few hundred dollars in profit per month for running a 24/7 webcam with new content generated each day.

LiveJournal: Snapshot Writing, Image Culture, and 'Friends'

Amanda's commitment to regularly chatting with her viewers illustrates the importance of popularity in the life of a camgirl. Online, popularity is established through social networks. Before 2000, camgirls used Usenet groups, Internet Relay Chat (IRC) spaces, and online bulletin boards to discuss their lives with their audiences. Later, they began communicating with their audiences via blogs. Among camgirls, LiveJournal remains the most popular of the blogging services. Camgirls were some of LiveJournal's earliest adopters, and their expressed needs helped shape the software used to run the service.[12]

Internet ethnographer Sherry Turkle has long maintained that we use our computers as "objects to think with."[13] In her 1995 book *Life on the Screen*, she observed that people conceptualize not just their computers, but *themselves* in terms of windows overlaid on a single screen. She argues that these conceptions represent a rejection of the modernist notion of a holistic self in favor of a postmodern view of identity as multiple, fractured, and segmented.[14] Examining testimony of many LiveJournal members has led me to believe that the webcam has likewise morphed into an evocative object for our age. As LiveJournal user Alby put it, "Posting to my journal is like taking a picture of inside, a record of how I feel at the moment that I am writing. If I don't write it, it is gone."[15]

Echoing Alby, LiveJournal user Scribble articulated his desire to write in his journal with a photographic analogy: "Do you ever see pictures of yourself that don't align with your idea of yourself?" Scribble asked. "Not necessarily better or worse—simply not right? Sometimes I think the journal is a textual claim that 'I look the way I think I look.' I dunno. For whatever jury exists."[16]

Just as the webcam delivers by-the-moment images of varying quality, 'snapshot writing' has more to do with timeliness than with craft. Most snapshot writing consists of quotidian remarks like, "This chicken salad I am eating is gross." Other times, a quick entry such as "I hate myself" hints at a desire for conversation with—or intervention by—others.

Just as it is difficult for professional photographers to give themselves over to the webcam, snapshot writing can be difficult for those who were raised to believe writing must be 'correct' and polished before it is released to the world. At first, I had much more difficulty engaging in snapshot writing than I did in webcamming my image to the world. I quickly realized that this is because I do not think of myself as a model or an actress, but I do think of myself as a writer with something to lose from releasing half-formed thoughts to the world.

I have gotten more comfortable with the form, mostly because my quick and unedited posts on LiveJournal tend to elicit many more responses than my longer, more well-thought-out ones. Although this dynamic sometimes baffles LiveJournal users, anyone who attends writers' groups knows that a short story with structural problems always gets more commentary than a polished manuscript. Similarly, teachers quickly realize that a tentative, open-ended question elicits more response from students than does a rigorous lecture. Snapshot writing presents itself as in-process and open to commentary from others. When I was working on my Ph.D. dissertation and needed immediate gratification, I would often post chapters on LiveJournal. Where my dissertation committee might take up to a month to comment on what I had written, I knew I could count on receiving comments from LiveJournal readers that same afternoon.

Like webcammers, LiveJournal users often supplement their texts with high-quality digital images, and sometimes even forego text altogether. For the generation of Web users who grew up with digital photography, this has been a boon. Others feel differently. Mia Lipner, who grew up using text-only bulletin board systems in cyberspace, feels that the LiveJournal bias of "reading more carefully the words of people who put images with their text" disturbingly mirrors her experience in the offline world as a blind woman. "People don't acknowledge my presence (waiters asking my friends what I want to order, etc.)," Mia explains, "not because they can't see me, but because I can't see them (or myself)."[17]

LiveJournal user Laura Fokkena agrees. "The first photo I posted of myself online" she says, "was a black and white scan of my driver's license, and that's what got all the commentary on my LiveJournal." Laura finds this dynamic frustrating. "I already know what I look like," she explains, "and whether someone likes or despises my image, well, there isn't much I can do about it. I *can* change my words, though, and that's where I'd like the response, attention, venomous critique or whatever to go."[18]

"The whole lookism thing has probably been talked to death, but I still want to bring it up," confessed LiveJournal user Helena Kvarnstrom:

> I can write some academic coursework essay on lesbian & gay culture and use big school words and no one says anything about it (good or bad). But the second I put up a half-naked picture I am flooded with comments both loving and hating it and there is an assumption that *I need help*, I need advice, and I am not really sure what I am doing.[19]

Yet even Helena sees the value in putting her work online. "Lookism makes me suspicious as to why so many people read my journal, why they comment, and that's a bit sad to me," she explains. At the same time, however, she points out:

> If this ridiculousness (which isn't really ridiculous because it is a strange and power-ful cultural situation, really, however fucked up) makes more people actually read some of my academic things and maybe become interested in feminist theory or whatever, that's very cool. I am not sure if that actually happens, but in idealistic moments I pretend it does.[20]

In addition to its snapshot-writing aesthetic and its obsession with the visual, LiveJournal is significant in the blogosphere for its capacity to connect users as 'friends'—a feature that is crucial to an understanding of the development of community among its members. I explore the dynamic of 'friending' at length in Chapter Five, but for now, here is a brief introduction: I join LiveJournal and create a page for myself. One day, "Suzy" leaves a comment in my journal. Because Suzy's LiveJournal is only a click away, I take a look. I find her writing style interesting and decide to add her to my Friends List. (Suzy may or may not reciprocate by adding me to her own Friends List, then or later.) From there on, each time Suzy updates her blog, her post turns up on my Friends Page.[21]

As a technological tool, the Friends List is not dissimilar to more recently developed syndication services such as RSS or AtomFeed. As a social mobilizer, the Friends List gives LiveJournal users a sense of community that is distinctly different from that shared by other types of bloggers. Researcher danah boyd points out that the thing that distinguishes users of sites like LiveJournal is their ability to demonstrate their "public displays of connection" to one another.[22] Viewers who want to see my friends on the system need only to "hop from one profile to another through a chain of Friendship."[23] Because the system allows for the organizing of people first and interests second, boyd explains, communities tend to be organized "egocentrically," with a user's Friends List constituting the audience she believes she is addressing when she writes.[24]

Assessing Web Popularity

Quantifying a camgirl's popularity is a complicated business. In 2001, cam-girl Ana Voog sent me some press quotes she had received over the years about her site, saying "You can see how they all get the story different or just plain wrong." At about that same time, the *New York Post* had credited Voog with receiving 700,000 visitors a day, while Goldmine put her traffic at 700,000 *hits* a day. The *Philadelphia Enquirer* said her site was "accessed a half-million times a day by people around the world," while *Der Spiegel* put daily traffic at "more than 200,000 people."[25]

This confusion stemmed in part from the fact that Web site viewership is measured in three different ways: hits, page views, and unique visitors. Technically, a hit refers to the access of any file on a Web page, so that a page with five images and two audio files would count as seven hits. Today, experts compare single page views, rather than hits, but even page views don't reveal how many people visit a site in a day. For this we need access to a camgirl's referrer logs, which track site visitors individually. These 'uniques' are the best indicators of Web viewership, but content providers tend to guard such figures closely. Without them it is impossible to determine whether a site's popularity reflects occasional vists from a broad viewership or intense attention from a small but obsessive fan base.[26]

I ran into these problems in my efforts to assess the influence of the JenniCam. I can personally attest to the popularity of the site: during the three days it linked to my homepage, I received more traffic than I had during the whole of the previous six months. When I tell someone about this project and they give me a quizzical look, I say, "Like the JenniCam." At this, they usually nod. They may not ever have seen the site, but they've heard of it.

And yet I still do not know how many visitors the JenniCam received. In 1998, Salon reported that Ringley claimed 100 million hits per week, which works out to approximately 14 million hits per day.[27] Three years later, in a personal conversation with Ringley's business manager, Jodi Anderson, I was told that the number was closer to 5 million per day.[28] Dividing 5 million hits by five (the number of images on the JenniCam's original splash page) tells us that the JenniCam received no more than 1 million page views per day, but I cannot extrapolate how many of those 1 million page views came from individual viewers. That information is private.[29]

Beyond audience numbers, other factors contribute to the perceived fame of a camgirl. In her heyday, Ana Voog received only 10,000 unique visitors a day, but becausee of the amount of press coverage she has received over the years she is widely regarded among those I've interviewed as the Web's second most popular camgirl.[30] I likewise gained press notoriety while webcamming full time, not because I had a million hits a day, but because as a girl-dissertating-on-webcams-with-her-own-webcam, I made for a good story. This media attention generated Web hits for me, thus creating my popularity after the fact.

Today, press fascination with social networking makes evaluating Web popularity even trickier. In 2007, singer Tila Tequila—dubbed 'The Madonna of MySpace' on the strength of her staggering 1.7 million MySpace friends—learned this lesson the hard way.[31] Heartened by press coverage of musical acts like the Arctic Monkeys and Lily Allen (both hailed for using MySpace to bolster their fan bases), Tequila thought she was in a good position to release her debut single online.[32] Tequila was so confident of the loyalty of her MySpace friends that she turned down record label offers to produce and publicize her work. Yet in the end just 13,000 people paid to download Tequila's single—less than one percent of her MySpace friends. The single didn't even show up on the Billboard Hot Digital Songs chart.

Toward a Theory of Micro-celebrity

Stories like Tequila's demonstrate the trouble with using terms like 'celebrity' to discuss popular Web personalities. As Horkheimer and Adorno made clear, celebrity and capital are inextricably linked in the modern age: indeed, the former exists to prop up the latter.[33] Yet in terms of both raw audience numbers and economic gain, Web stars pale in comparison to even 'D List' performers in the film, television and music industries. While the Web can be used as a platform for traditional celebrity—Tila Tequila was recently hired by MTV to appear in her own show—it cannot create old-fashioned stars of its own. Instead, the Web provides the conditions for what I call 'micro-celebrity.'

"In the future," musician and blogger Momus once quipped, "everyone will be famous to fifteen people."[34] In the spirit of Momus (himself a 'star' on LiveJournal), micro-celebrity is best understood as a new style of online performance that involves people 'amping up' their popularity over the Web using technologies like video, blogs and social networking sites. Micro-celebrity sometimes looks like conventional celebrity, but the two aren't the same.

According to film theorist Richard Dyer, Hollywood celebrity turns on questions of reality versus image. "The whole media construction of stars encourages us to think of 'really,'" Dyer says.[35] As P. David Marshall puts it, the audience for celebrity "obsessively and incessantly asks, 'what is Marilyn Monroe "really" like? Is Paul Newman "really" the way he appears in his films?'" Television celebrities are expected to be slightly less aloof than their film counterparts, but the business of 'really' remains an issue.[36]

Consider the famous 1970's commercial where American actor Robert Young says, "I'm not a doctor, but I play one on TV." When it has its desired effect, Young's statement translates to, "I'm not really a doctor, even though I play one on *Marcus Welby, M.D.* That's not a problem though, because I really *am* a celebrity. Hopefully, you will identify with me (consciously or not) and as a result, you will choose to purchase the drug I am endorsing."

Unlike film and television audiences, Web viewers don't seem particularly interested in purchasing products endorsed by Web stars. Instead, their interest takes an ethical turn: rather than speculating on who a Web personality "really is," viewers tend to debate the personality's obligations to those who made her *what* she is. This is because on the Web, popularity depends upon a connection to one's audience, rather than an enforced separation from them. "Most people in technoculture know full well that they aren't really celebrities," explains Jodi Dean. "In fact, this anxiety about not being known, this tension between the conviction that one is known and not known, is a key component of the celebrity mode of subjectivization."[37]

Dean's observation explains why a camgirl will explain, in one breath, how she is in no way similar to a film or television star and yet insist in the next that because she opens her life to public scrutiny, she's not an 'ordinary' person either. Often, she'll describe her viewers as 'family,' encouraging people to relate to her, while insisting that she remains misunderstood by everyone who watches her or reads her writing. Always, she'll negotiate what she means—both as a person and as a product—with those who see themselves as her customers, her friends, her detractors, or her neighbors on the Web.

Viewers find themselves subject to similar contradictions. A viewer may profess to hate camgirls, seeing them as contrived and attention seeking, yet find herself defending one particular camgirl as 'the real deal.' A viewer may send fan mail to a camgirl he idolizes, only to get return mail asking for a job reference. Viewers at work may travel to what they expect to be a 'clean' Web site, only to discover it houses pornographic material. Alternately, they may expect pornography and receive none. Finally, a viewer may watch in horror, as I did, the webcammed suicide attempt of someone with whom they converse every day, but have no home address to give to the police. In short, relationships between camgirls and viewers feel 'real' (which is to say, simulated) until suddenly—and often without warning—they turn real.

Postmodern Branding

In spite of their differences, Web micro-celebrities share something important with mainstream media stars: both must brand or die. During the period of actor Brad Pitt's infidelities, young women started declaring themselves (sometimes only half-jokingly) to be members of 'Team Aniston' or 'Team Jolie.' Similarly, viewers who respond to Ana Voog's performance art persona might not care for Amanda's All American Girl look, though they might be intrigued by my Academic Camgirl schtick. As ever, identification says more about the viewer than the viewed. In his research of user profiles on MySpace, Hugo Liu found that the interests people listed tended to cluster in "rich motifs like irony, alienation, utopia, and satire." Liu pointed out that rather than factual declaration of interests, profile listings were better understood as 'taste performances'—or what I have been calling brands.[38]

Branding wasn't always related to consumer identity issues in this way. Until the 1950's, advertisers tended to build brands either by extolling the luxury they promised (e.g., automobile and alcohol ads) or by communicating quasi-scientific data, as in the famous American chewing gum commercial that boasted that "Four out five dentists surveyed recommend Trident sugarless gum for their patients who chew gum." In *The Conquest of Cool*, Thomas Frank demonstrates how identity-oriented branding techniques emerged in the 1960's, when students frustrated with the Vietnam War began to take jobs with advertising agencies.[39] The students-turned-employees quickly realized that consumers coming into adulthood post-Vietnam perceived most advertisements as both dull and 'part of the problem'—inconsistent, that is, with their countercultural ideals. In response, advertisers began creating campaigns with putatively anti-establishment messages like "7UP: The Uncola" and Volkswagen's classic: "How often do you buy a new car? That's too often."

Douglas Holt uses the term "postmodern brand" to describe advertising marked by its use of irony and its association with subcultural identity, among other things.[40] The 'modern' Trident gum featured dentists in its ads. Today, a trip to Tridentgum.com. features "Little Mouth," a set of animated wind-up dentures that fetches products with names like Tropical Twist and Green Apple Fusion.[41] How Trident was talked into using dentures as a mascot is anyone's guess.

It is important to realize that postmodern branding engages in the appearance of countercultural critique, rather than its enactment. It doesn't much matter that our Macs help us "think different" if our actions don't reflect those thoughts. Likewise, consuming the anti-establishment aesthetic

Figure 5. Branding the Suicide Girls. From the "Tour" section of the site at http://suicidegirls.com/tour

of a site like The Suicide Girls (which bills itself as "naked, punk, indie, emo and goth") is not the same as participating in those subcultures—although it might arguably lead to participation at some point down the road.[42]

Ten years ago, I might have forwarded the URL for Trident's Small Mouth to some friends. Now I wonder if only children are supposed to be looking at the Trident site. Part of our fatigue as consumers has to do with the rise of digital production and distribution tools over the last decade. Software like Photoshop, GarageBand and iMovie now make it possible for talented amateurs to create photographs, musical tracks and videos that are on par with those made by professionals, while Web-based delivery systems like iTunes and YouTube make it possible to distribute one's work to the masses.

Douglas Holt argues that purveyors of postmodern brands today find themselves in the same situation as their modern brand predecessors: consumers now perceive them as dated, and don't feel compatible with the ideologies behind them. At least as an aesthetic, counterculture is waning, irony is old, and *verite* (in real or faux form) is corporate. Everyone knows real amateurs are busy polishing their productions, not scuffing them up. Consumers, no longer bothered about the presence of advertising in their lives, now willingly volunteer (or are paid low wages) to engage in labor that was once the domain of the advertiser. Many of my students in East London have already been conscripted into 'street teams' and charged with 'virusing' promotional objectives for companies like Sony and Nike.

When I ask these students whether they see such work as exploiting, for instance, subcultural practices within hip hop, I get two answers. The first is that on good days, they see themselves as ambassadors representing the buying concerns of their peers. The second is that someone is going to get paid to do it—why not them? I get similar answers when I ask students how they feel about the fact that Microsoft has bought the right to data mine their Facebook profiles. They are not uncritical about capitalist expansion into their data space, but they believe that it is inevitable, and that it is a waste of their time to fight it. Interestingly, many of my students perk right up when they discover that they might stand to profit by using things like Google AdSense on their own blogs. Rather than dismissing this response as shallow or greedy, I find it interesting to re-frame it as a desire to gain back some of their lost agency in a networked age.

The Case of the Lonely Girl

In September of 2006, I came across a story that seemed to me to sum all the aspects of theatrical authenticity, celebrity and branding that had begun with Jennifer Ringley's camera a decade earlier. The *New York Times* gave the story front-page play and a mysterious title: "The LonelyGirl That

Wasn't."[43] The article told the story of Bree, a beautiful young woman who posted under the name 'LonelyGirl15.' Bree, who presented herself as a home-schooled fifteen-year-old with penchants for stuffed animals and boys with computers, released a series of videos (shot mainly in her bedroom) that quickly became the obsession of "millions" of viewers.

From the beginning of Bree's broadcasts, skeptics found it difficult to swallow the idea that a child with 'strict religious parents' who was routinely confined to her room also had access to a camera and computer with which to regularly update a personal video site. Cynics suggested that the idea of a supermodel-pretty girl who routinely quoted Richard Feynman was a little too geek-good to be true. And it was. As *Times* writers Virginia Heffernan and Tom Zellner Jr. reported, the collective efforts of Web viewers led to the identification of Bree as "Jessica Rose, a 20-ish ... graduate of the New York Film Academy."[44] To make matters worse, it turned out that the entire project was intended as an early run for what would eventually become a Hollywood movie.

In keeping with industry trends, the bulk of coverage regarding Lonely-Girl15 occurred not in the pages of the *Times* itself, but in a *Times*-sponsored blog entitled "Screens." The day the story broke, Heffernan asked readers, "Does the revelation of LonelyGirl15's true identity as an actress change the way you will interpret amateur video online?"[45]

Anyone who has been on the Web for a month knows that the quickest way to get people to respond to you online is to ask a question that allows them to say "No." Out of nearly one hundred and fifty responses to Heffernan's query, only a handful admitted to having been taken in by the LonelyGirl hoax. Many posters shared the sentiments of Karen, who asked, "Why dispel something so harmless? No one was injured because a few young adults wanted to get movie contracts or break into the business, and thousands of people were entertained."

Occasionally, someone questioned Karen's idea that the LonelyGirl15 stunt was harmless. Noting that young people comprised a large section of YouTube's viewship, a few posters asked whether the creators ever responded to the many teens following Bree online. Other posters noted the sense of community that had developed around the show during its run. A user named Scorched Hot Tub explained that Bree's videos inspired "a host of response videos—some earnest, some dismissive and others purely farcical."[46]

Finally, a large number of people seemed to object to the LonelyGirl15 story running on the front page of the *Times'* print newspaper. Poster S. Dog summed up the sentiments of many:

> The *NY Times* is the old gray lady (and I mean that as a compliment). Seeing her pander to the garbage that gets shown at YouTube is like seeing your favorite

aunt making a fool of herself at a frat party. You just want to go up to her, grab her handbag, and say, "You're too old for this. I'm taking you home."[47]

As a forty-something academic writing about youth culture and the Web, I can attest that the *Times* isn't the only gray lady who has been told to go home before she embarrasses herself any further. The reason I stay is because today's Web viewers, like the Screens posters, seem to understand something with which both reporters and academics still struggle: it is time to get over our preoccupation with the reality effects of new media, and begin the long and difficult work of understanding how Web-based communication affects politics, economics and ethics—both online and off.

When 1970's feminists insisted that the personal was political, they didn't mean 'sort of political,' or 'political, but not political like war.' In the same vein, I want to urge resistance to sentiments like those of poster Pravin Shah Jr., who responded to the LonelyGirl story by writing, "Sixty-five bodies were found in Iraq today. And YOU are spending time on this? Attempt to get a life, folks."[48] The first problem I have with a statement like this is that it implies that one must choose to be concerned with either the war or with LonelyGirl. The truth is, there are enough pages in the newspaper, and time enough in our day, for both stories. Since Plato, people have worried that citizens cannot be simultaneously interested in popular culture and questions of peace and civil liberties. Since Plato, these people have been wrong.

The second disturbing element of Shah's words lies in the charge, "Attempt to get a life, folks." As someone who studies online culture I hear this sort of thing quite a bit, so much so that I now process it as word salad. Get a life. Attempt to get a life. Get real. Get reality. Attempt to get reality. Whose reality? Jean Baudrillard once infamously wrote that the first Gulf War did not happen.[49] He was referring to the levels of media-enabled simulation that made it impossible to experience the war as anything but an extended exercise in hyperreality. Is this new war—which 'embeds' reporters into its machinations and helps propel multiplayer Web games like America's Army—any different? Maybe Baudrillard is right, and like an advertising-free world, reality is something we can't get anymore, no matter how much we attempt it. Does this mean there is nothing left to do?

Perhaps there is a way to get out of the reality morass by doubling back the way we got in it: through consumption. When Shah accuses us of "spending time on this," his objective is to shame us by calling us bad consumers. Good revolutionary shoppers know there is only so much time to spend, and we are wasting it. But what if I take a page from my street-team students and think of my time not in terms of consumption, but of labor? I will never be optimistic enough to think my time labor can progressively influence large corporations like Sony or Nike, or the US Army, but I might be willing to believe that the labor I spend making connections with others online is an investment, rather than a waste.

Another way to put this is to say that I believe in the power of micropolitics. Political scientist William Connolly defines micropolitics as local conversations and actions in nonpolitical arenas that "set the stage for macro politics by rendering people receptive or unreceptive to certain messages and plans of action."[50] The dinner table is a micropolitical arena, as are the movie theatre, the bathroom, the club, the gym, the doctor's office, the pages of a magazine, the lyrics of a song, and yes—the World Wide Web. In the next chapter I discuss how the micropolitical symbol of the camgirl might be reconceptualized in the service of macropolitical aims.

2. I'd Rather be a Camgirl than a Cyborg: The Future of Feminism on the Web

In the dream, I hold a mirrored sphere the size of a basketball in my hands. I throw the sphere against a clear wall. Thump, it goes. Each time it bounces, I see parts of myself reflected, refracted. "It's impossible to see it all," I reason. "Nobody can see it all." Thump. Thump.

I open my eyes, squinting at the mop of pink hair. Stacy Pershall of Atomcam rolls over and yawns but shows no signs of waking.[1] In the other bed, Eric Durchholz of PlanetConcrete snores.[2]

Thump. Thump. The pounding continues, and a voice comes through the door.

"Hola! Hello! Room service. Can we clean now?"

The year is 2001. Stacy, Eric, and I are staying at the Omni Hotel in Austin, Texas, attending the SXSW New Media Conference. Later that week, we are scheduled to speak on a panel called "Everything you ever wanted to know about webcamming, but were afraid to ask."[3] All night, we had joked about the title of the panel. There seemed to be nothing our viewers were afraid to ask us, and nothing we were afraid to tell. "Queens of the over-share," Eric pronounced us, his twangy laugh indicating he included himself as a princess among the royalty present. We were supposed to meet with Amanda of Amandacam[4] and a camgirl I'll call Allie—aybe they could help us figure out what we could possibly say to our viewers that they didn't already know. Fighting my worst hangover in years, I open the hotel door a quarter inch to talk to the maid on the other side. "Can you come back?" I ask. "We are sleeping."

"Yes, okay, yes. How much time you need?" She waits as I turn from the door. Overflowing ashtrays compete with empty beer bottles. In the corner, a half-gallon of Stacy's Manic Panic pink hair dye spoils a pile of formerly white towels. "Conferences are sort of a Spring Break for adults," my friend Morgan had recently joked. I don't feel particularly adult right now.

"We probably won't need a maid today," I answer, smelling onions from last night's room service. When had we ordered room service?

The maid is not pleased. "Hang this up." She hands me a plastic sign that hooks onto the doorknob. The sign reads, "Only a goldfish can live without privacy."

Only a goldfish. Before I stumble back to bed, I check to see whether our mobile camera is still broadcasting. It is. Earlier in the evening, it had been uploading images of me gossiping with Eric. Later, it had broadcasted pictures of an SXSW party we attended, where I am pretty sure someone jumped in a bubble bath for the camera at some point. For the past few hours, it had been watching the three of us sleep.

As a reflex, I check in on my friends on LiveJournal.[5] There, I see Allie's public apology-in-advance for not attending our conference panel for which she was supposed to be a speaker. Thus far, nobody responding to Allie's journal had asked whether she had informed *us* of her decision not to come. (She hadn't.) Back in bed, I wait for the spins to stop while my mind reels off a list of questions: What type of person apologizes online in a public forum before contacting those directly affected?[6] And why am I already planning my own public LiveJournal response to Allie's apology, rather than calling her on the telephone? What are we all doing, broadcasting our lives to utter strangers on the Web while hiding from the peering eyes of Latina maids in the morning?

Although this story represents an exceptional day in the life of a camgirl, I tell it because it illuminates a set of recurring themes. First, there is the theme of reflectivity, with webcams serving as mirrors for those who choose to display themselves to the world in this way. Next is reflexivity, the way our dialectical exchanges place us in a continual feedback loop with others. Finally, there is the theme of refraction, which occurs when one person's definition of public is another's definition of private or professional, as in my reaction to Allie's posting to her blog before contacting us.

In the previous chapter, I discussed the ways in which camgirls deploy theatrical authenticity and celebrity in their presentation of self-as-brand. This chapter explores what it means to declare oneself (or be declared by others) a camgirl—a symbol people often love, or love to hate. "Maybe it's just me," confessed Lisa Batey, formerly of the cam-house HereandNow, "but when I mention I was a camgirl, people get this look on their face that causes me to spew explanations."[7] After years of interviews—and eighteen months spent in front of the camera myself—I can say with confidence that it's not just Lisa.

From Digital Drag to Gender Performativity

My first exposure to camgirls came after I had spent nearly a decade in online environments. When I first went online in the early 1990's, people were fascinated by what I call 'digital drag': performances in which people (almost always men) attempted to represent themselves in cyberspace as something other than their offline gender, sexuality, race, or ability. Back then, the notion that "On the Internet, nobody knows you're a dog" (to quote the caption of a well-known *New Yorker* cartoon) was particularly attractive to those limited by sexism, racism, ageism, and disability discrimination in the offline world. That said, digital drag was never restricted solely to society's 'others.' The idea of the Internet as a liminal space had broad mainstream appeal to all sorts of users. Internet ethnographer Sherry Turkle even lauded the practice as a way to work through postmodern ideas of the self. [8]

Yet almost as soon as digital drag arose, feminists began to question the belief that online identity play was as progressive an activity as its proponents declared. Cyberspace ethnographer Lisa Nakamura demonstrated how users given the option of being 'anything' online often opted to drag racist and sexist roles such as subservient geishas and overaggressive samurai. [9] Nakamura's critique of "identity tourism" on the Net echoed earlier feminist scholarship on sex tourists who often understand their activities as 'naughty fun' rather than as commercialized exercises of power, in part because of the far-from-home locales in which they transpire.

Another critique of digital drag was that it obscured the fact that *all* identity is performative, as Judith Butler would say. [10] When introducing my students to the concept of performativity, I often explain to them that although I may have a computer, I cannot *have* the Internet, because the Internet is not a thing, but rather the effect of multiple networked performances among computers, phones, cable, satellites, and power lines. Likewise, I can have a body, but I cannot *have* a gender or race, because these are the result of a series of networked performances among doctors, families, communities, judges, and so forth. And just as the average Internet user does not see how her Google search result comes from the exchange of billions of bits of information flowing between cooperating computers, we rarely notice the ways gender and race is embedded within culture, because its end result—the 'having' of it—strikes us as transparent, intuitive, and natural. Yet identity is hardly natural. If it were, we wouldn't spend our days validating who we are with our clothing, makeup, photos, sound clips, iPod playlists, working papers, and cross-referenced, interactive blogs.

In 1994, I joined a New York City–based text-only bulletin board called Echo, which at the time was unique in having a large percentage of women as users. In 1996, with Echo founder Stacy Horn, I co-edited a special issue of the journal *Women and Performance*, entitled "Sexuality and Cyberspace: Performing the Digital Body." [11] In that journal, I co-wrote an essay with a transgendered woman named Kaley Davis, who was having more luck passing as a woman offline than online.[12] In everyday life, her clothing choices, hair styles, and body shape made the switch from Ken to Kaley unmistakable. Online, Kaley was—like the rest of us—nothing more than the words she typed on the screen. Because she had joined Echo as Ken, users—particularly female ones—were reluctant to accept her as the woman she now claimed to be.

From Essentialism to Everyday Cyborg Feminism

At the end of the essay Kaley and I wrote, I voiced a hope that feminists might turn their attention to how gender performativity figured in the lives of biological women performing as women on the Internet, a focus of this book. Of course, scholars have been writing about women online for nearly a decade now, beginning with female head counts in cyberspace,[13] moving to analyses of the ways in which men and women communicate in digital forums,[14] and continuing with critiques of women online grounded in questions of race, class, and nation.[15] Unfortunately, many 'women in' studies of cyberspace commit the same error as proponents of digital drag: they assume offline identity to be material rather than performative. Such is the downside of using a static and unchanging term—such as 'woman,' 'feminine,' or even 'the body'—to describe something that is actually the result of a number of fluctuating conditions. As Ellen Rooney explains, "Feminisms return to the problem of essentialism—despite their shared distaste for the mystifications of Woman—because it remains difficult to engage in feminist analysis and politics if not 'as a woman.'"[16]

But these days, it is difficult to determine what constitutes *any* body, let alone a woman's. Here, I am rehearsing Donna Haraway's argument that even the most 'natural' body is a cyborg: one both organic and technological.[17] In 1984, Haraway helped a generation of feminists to definitively reject essentialist notions of what women 'are' by arguing that bodies, machines, geographies, genders, and sexualities co-determine one another's meanings in a dialectical fashion. "By the late twentieth century, our time, a mythic time," she wrote, "we are all chimeras, theorized and fabricated hybrids of machine and organism; in short, we are cyborgs."[18]

One of the most moving pieces on everyday cyborg life I have ever read is Sharon Lehner's essay "My Womb, the Mosh Pit," which we published in *Sexuality and Cyberspace*.[19] In fiercely intimate detail, Sharon described how she was introduced to, made familiar with, and ultimately separated from the fetus of her unborn child, entirely through sonogram images. Certain moments of that story—for example, the nurse's declaration that Sharon's fetus had a penis that was "standing like the Statue of Liberty"—still resonate with me as examples of the power of gender performativity. Others, such as Sharon's lament that she was "mourning the death of an image," remind me of cyborg theorist Sandy Stone's comment that asking whether mediated identities are real is similar to "asking where the flame goes once a candle is blown out."[20]

Like performativity, cyborg theory helps destabilize feminism's too-easy dependence on identity politics. Whereas theories of performativity articulate epistemological propositions (explaining how we come to know something as true), the figure of the cyborg offers us ontological insights regarding the technological nature of our bodily existence. As Haraway's famous query "Why should our bodies end at the skin?" indicates, cyborg ontology allows affinities beyond the real, or even the human.

Enter the JenniCam

Though "Sexuality and Cyberspace" received favorable notices, one review jarred me by singling out my writing as "pedestrian." Given my self-proclaimed interest in the everyday, I tried to take that as my due. But when those same reviewers summed up the banal side of the Web with a reference to "stale, stolen moments visiting JenniCam," I felt an involuntary swell of solidarity.[21]

Despite the fact that the JenniCam was by that time being uniformly heralded as the "next big thing" in cyberspace, I had never visited the site myself. Most of my online experiences had been on a text-based bulletin board system entirely free of images and advertisements. Although I maintained my own homepage on the Web and even had a part-time job working for Prodigy Corporation's Web division, I considered these to be economic gestures rather than social ones. To be honest, given all the purported possibilities for women to refashion the meaning of gender in cyberspace, the JenniCam struck me as retrograde in the extreme. First, I was put off by the notion of a public sphere propelled not by topics such as movies or politics, but by a single personality. Second, I had trouble wrapping my mind around the site's promise of 24/7 voyeurism. This didn't quite seem like using the master's tools to dismantle the master's house.[22]

Yet because Jennifer and I were now yoked together, my own narcissism was tweaked—anyone these reviewers disliked as much as they disliked me might be worth viewing. I typed the URL and watched a webcammed image of a living room refreshing every few minutes. Jennifer wasn't even home. The whole thing came across as an exercise in deferred gratification, with an endless expectation that something might happen. Waiting for the webcam to display something besides her empty couch, I browsed the JenniCam's archived photos and online journals. The moment I figured out that I could match the date and time stamps on the photos to the journal entries, I was hooked. In viewing the images as a narrative, I was getting an inkling of who Jennifer was, and why she might find it useful to share her life with the world. When she finally did appear, I found myself jumping back and forth between her new webcammed images and the archived images and journals.

Like any good consumer, I also clicked on the links that Jennifer provided to other camgirls in her branding efforts. Some of these camgirls were operating in the style of Ringley, others clearly were not. After a few weeks of surfing, I was able to categorize the homecamming of that period into five major groups: the real-life cam, the art cam, the porn cam, the group house cam, and the community cam.

The Real-life Camgirl

The JenniCam's "real-life" approach was a model for other webcammers and still defines the genre in the minds of many. "I first had a single camera in my single dorm room," Jennifer recalled. "The room was roughly eight feet by twelve feet, extremely small."[23] Given the size of her space, it was quite possible for Ringley to attempt to show everything on camera in her early days; however, from the very beginning only certain parts of her life were visible to viewers. For example, although she included shots of herself having sex in the bedroom (because "people have sex in real life"), Ringley consciously chose not train a camera on the toilet. Still, the JenniCam's aesthetic influenced thousands of imitators. A quick look at justin.tv's 'featured channels', for example, shows how the site has managed to mix 'reality ideology,' micro-celebrity, and streaming video technology to create JenniCams for a new era.

The Artist Camgirl

Not every homecam hewed to the reality ideology like the JenniCam and its spin-offs. Ana Voog's AnaCam site warns viewers, "Sometimes [my webcam] is more about showing you what is going on INSIDE me than what is going on in my actual physical surroundings. That is why I like to … be playful with this medium."[24] Ana began her webcam in 1997. As she likes to remind me, "I was the seventh camgirl, and the first to call webcamming art!" Here is how camgirl Stacy Pershall described her first encounter with Ana's site:

> There was this bowl with fresh plums in it. The camera was trained on the plums, but I knew someone (Ana?) was eating them, because every few minutes, a pit would replace one of the plums in the bowl. I watched, transfixed, as the bowl of purple plums turned into a bowl of brown pits. It sounds odd now, but to

me, this was a "Fluxus moment"—this is when I decided, "I need to do this for myself."[25]

I thought I would like the AnaCam, given Stacy's description. Yet I confess to having hated what I saw when I first stopped by: a photo of a dog resting on a couch, shot with some type of blue filter, refreshing periodically. Next to that was a photo collage of Ana, an undernourished white-haired pixie woman, striking arty poses: Ana licking a window; Ana's eyeball; Ana with headphones on; Ana with a pair of scissors across her pubis; Ana's hands, folded in prayer. "Wow," I thought to myself. "Art school corrupts absolutely."

I started looking around the site. There were hundreds of pages to read, thousands of images to look at, and several bulletin boards and chat rooms in which to participate. "She sure does put work into this stuff, for what that's worth," I recall thinking, clicking on a link to her public bulletin board. This is where I got my first real taste of what I've come to think of as Ana-speak:

> what i wouldn't give for REAL breasts!!!! u have infinite shapes to be! bullet bra, push up bra, etc. mine are ONE shape. they do not MOVE, or JIGGLE! ... i mean I am very happy i had them done, and I don't regret it ... but it's still a self-conscious thing that when i hug people, i wonder if they are noticing how hard my breasts are and wondering what's up with that ...[26]

As stylistically bizarre as I initially thought they were, Ana Voog's journal entries demonstrated just how many false assumptions one can make based

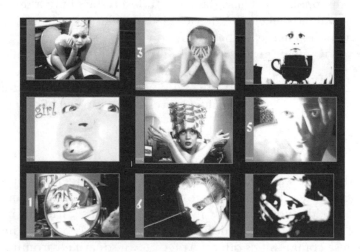

Figure 6. Best of AnaCam. Courtesy Ana Voog.

on images alone. A native Minnesotan, Voog never went to art school. As the post quoted above details, Ana has extremely large breast implants, and often wears a T-shirt that says, "Yes, they are fake." Over the years, I have come to know Ana Voog as an artist and a friend. I've seen her demonstrate self-developed webcam techniques to established artists in New York, helped her debate street harassment with strangers stopping by her site, and noticed her encouraging a generation of younger girls to express themselves over the Web. What I originally dismissed as affectation, I have now come to understand as one woman's determination to take the phrase 'life as art' quite literally.

The Porn Camgirl

As Jennifer Ringley was making her life cam and Ana Voog was making her art cam, the commercial pornography industry was finding its own webcamming niche. The single most successful woman to mix the aesthetics of pinup-girl culture with homepages was Danni Ashe, a former exotic dancer who began her Danni's Hard Drive site in 1995 as a way to continue her fan club and sell her videos.[27] With her cornfed, big-breasted looks and her 'Welcome to my Web site: Here are my sexy friends!' demeanor, Ashe still maintains an impressive archive of still images on her site, and plenty of downloadable prerecorded videos.

It is now commonplace to find adult film and magazine stars supplementing their income or boosting their fan base through Web sites of their own. Yet viewers hoping to see their favorite adult entertainers live on camera will be disappointed. These days, if adult web stars have a site boasting a camera, it will most likely shuttle viewers to satellite sites featuring anonymous women who charge by the minute for private shows.

Other early camgirls were not adult film stars but sexually explicit artists who mixed life, art, and porn into their webcammed performances. Kristie Alshaibi (known online as ArtVamp) and Melissa Gira (discussed in Chapter Four) see themselves as sexual transgressors in the age of new media.[28]

Cam-community Girls

In much the same way that America Online taught a generation of users to surf the Web easily, homecam-communities such as StickCam,[29] WebcamNow,[30] and the now-defunct CitizenX[31] provide user-friendly interfaces for people with minimal technical skills who want to broadcast themselves online. These communities offer a type of town-square environment previously lacking in the webcamming world. On CitizenX, for example, viewers were urged both to "see whose spots are popular" and to "buy a cam, so we can see your face!" Of course, there are still more people watching than broadcasting on cam-communities. At CitizenX, the viewers-to-viewed ratio was generally around 4:1. Compared with a traditional homecam site such as JenniCam, though, this change was substantial.

The Cam-house Girl

Concurrent with the growing popularity of MTV's *Real World*, a series of 'cam-houses' popped up in the late 1990's. Unlike other camgirls, women in these cam-houses served as on-air talent rather than self-producers, although they may have been nominally involved in the technical and financial side of running the site. Most camgirls broadcast in silent, still images, but women on cam-house sites were usually featured in streaming format—that is, with full-motion audio and video. The expense of streaming meant that cam-houses like HereandNow had either corporate sponsorship or private funds, which tended to dry up quickly.[32] As a means of raising income, a cam-house would sometimes choose to feature pornography and charge a subscription to viewers.

Figure 7. WebcamNow community site. Clockwise from upper left: a list of all live webcams on the site, a webcammed image of the author in her "room," a list of all the chatters in the room, a listing of all the other possible chat rooms viewers can visit. Eagle-eyed readers will note the requisite "take off shirt" request made by someone in the "live chat" section. Courtesy WebcamNow.

Figure 8. The HereandNow house. The woman featured in "Stream 1" is Lisa Batey. Courtesy Erik Vidal.

Gay Male Cams

The preceding five genres were predominately female (although there were and are also male examples of each), but there is a sixth genre of webcamming that is specific to men alone: the gay male cam. In 1996, Timo at DefyMyCategory became the first camguy star.[33] Sean Patrick of the now defunct Seanpatricklive came next.[34] As former camguy star Eric Durchholz explains, "In the beginning, there weren't that many of us, and gay men were voracious in their appetite."[35] Unfortunately, the scene quickly fell prey to financial bickering. "Most gay men thought guy-cams should be free," Durchholz recalls, remembering accusations of "scams, fraud and other such nasty stuff." Today, reality-based homecamming featuring men exists only in small pockets on the Web. Durchholz explains, "These days, the guy-cam community consists mainly of former or current models or porn stars hanging out at home nude, or in 'whole house' situations where a bunch of off-duty frat boys supplement their tuition by hanging out in chat rooms on gay.com."

Why do Women Webcam?

I am often asked why camgirls choose to broadcast their lives to strangers. As an academic, I always have a ready explanation for why I chose to put myself in front of the camera: "It was for research. No, really." But other camgirls answer that question in divergent ways.

For the most famous camgirl—Jennifer Ringley—the webcam was meant to serve as a part of a social experiment. On her Web site, Ringley told her viewers that her cam was, "to put it most simply, a sort of window into a virtual human zoo":

> I don't sing or dance or do tricks (well, sometimes I do, but not very well and solely for my own amusement, not yours). By the same token, JenniCam is

virtually unedited and uncensored … So feel free to watch, or not, as you see fit. I am not here to be loved or hated, I am simply here to be me. [36]

For some camgirls, the primary thrill of running a webcam site was a technical one. Stacy Pershall once confessed that her most sexually arousing moment in homecamming was the day she got all her cameras running for the first time. "I was pretty charged up that day," she remembered. "I felt pretty macho."[37] Others, like Amanda from Amandacam, thought of what they did as community building. As she put it:

I spend between two and three hours a day in my chat room. My viewers aren't nameless and faceless to me, if they don't want to be. We have a community. I know who my viewers are, and they know I know. [38]

While most camgirls insist they aren't entertainers, others are quite happy to accept that moniker. Cera Byer of SeeMeScreaming added her homecam and a LiveJournal to her site in order to "give people a chance to watch me laboring," composing at her keyboard, practicing her violin, or writing song lyrics. Though she began her homecam as a marketing tool, Cera concedes that now it is an integral part of her overall art-making. "I've invited people into the process of creating," she explains, and viewers have responded by sending Cera mail to tell her "they've watched me working, looked through my artwork, and admire and respect what I am doing." Many viewers also send Cera their art to look over, in a sort of exchange of creative ideas. "I never expected that," admits Cera, "but I love it."[39]

Some women, including Auriea Harvey, use their webcams as a means to speak back to the new media industry. Harvey is an internationally known digital artist with indisputable talent for making beautiful images. Nevertheless, she insists on broadcasting herself from a tiny, grainy 'work cam.' Issues of global production and consumption have long featured heavily in Auriea's art; accordingly, she maintains her homecam to demonstrate that "technology doesn't make the Net; people do."[40]

Like Auriea's, camgirl Ana Voog's webcam began as a reaction to the media world. "I had so much trouble with record companies," explained Voog, who has recorded albums for Sony. "I had a pissy argument [with Sony] about the fact that I wanted input into my image, so they gave me a video cam and said 'Make some videos and we'll see what you've got.' Like it was 'cam homework' or something!" She continues:

I made my site, and I called [Sony] up and said, "By the way, I am on the Net 24 hours a day. There's your cam homework." And it was just my way of saying, "[screw] you" to the industry. You want pictures of me? You want to categorize

me, and figure out who I am? Then watch me sleep, watch me eat, watch me take
a shower, watch me be depressed, watch me do everything. Tune in.[41]

A number of women view their homecams as vehicles through which to
experiment with personae online. Many of these experiments, including
those of Kristie Alshaibi (known online as ArtVamp), intentionally blur distinctions between art, life and porn. Kristie originally conceived her homecam as a complement to a feature film she was shooting called *Other People's
Mirrors*. Among other things, the film tells the story of a woman named
Echo who has an erotic relationship with technological devices.

As Kristie describes it, the EchoCam was a carefully controlled environment in which performances were staged for public viewing. In contrast, the
VampCam was an unedited life cam that watched Kristie being a student or
a film director and entertaining her lovers. Art began to bleed into life once
Kristie wound up playing the role of Echo in her own film while working as
an escort to pay bills. Still, in Kristie's mind, Echo is a sexually glamorous
character, whereas ArtVamp is an everyday person, and their homecams are
designed to reflect as much.

Although many people associate webcams with the desire to make
pornography, many camgirls produce no sexual content at all. Andrea
Mignolo, formerly of HereandNow, resents the word 'porn' being used
to describe her time on her webcam. "Just because some women do porn,
doesn't mean that I do, or that I have to."[42] Anabella, the "JenniCam of
Argentina," says she has no problems with porn personally, but won't
engage in nudity on camera because of her children. "Here porn is not
legal," she explains, "but the Net is so universal, that if children want to
find it, they will."

As was common for many non-porn camgirls of the time, Anabella's site
began with the question, "Did you come here looking for sex?" She then
provided links to a number of explicit sites viewers could visit. "Believe it
or not, once I put up those links I get less requests to get naked!" Anabella
explained. "I think it's because people know that I will not do it, but I'll give
them the right place to find it. Besides, those links give me money."[43]

In sum, the answer to "Why webcam?" ranges from to a curiosity about
'reality' online, to technological interest, to the desire to make an artistic
statement of sorts, to a practical means to gain career exposure, to a means
of challenging one's image in a particular work environment, to experi-
mentation with personae. Sometimes the motivation stems from an interest
in pornography; other times, not. Yet as camgirl Jennifer Ringley remarks,
"People will take [cam sites] the way they choose to take them. For some it
will look like a means to self-validation, for some it will look like an artistic
canvas, for some it will look like a tarty competitive display."[44]

Are Webcams Voyeuristic?

It is common to hear camgirl spectatorship described as voyeuristic, but is this term really applicable? Orthodox psychology defines voyeurism as a sexual fetish in which an unseen viewer spies on an unsuspecting body that is "naked, in the process of disrobing, or engaging in sexual activity."[45] The term enjoys a wider usage among the general public: a search for 'voyeur' on Google yielded over 24 million hits, directing viewers to Web sites of widely differing content, yielding differing viewer responses. The fact that some of these hits represent actual voyeurism, while most represent simulated voyeurism, can be cause for confusion. People feel understandably anxious after reading stories about 'Peeping Toms' who have begun posting their footage of unsuspecting victims on sites like YouTube. Yet while orthodox voyeurism exists online, most commercial 'upskirt' cam sites primarily draw on footage from paid sex workers. Just as the porn industry has mastered the production and manufacture of 'amateur' sex, so too has it mastered presentations of what only appears to be voyeurism.

Many people use the word 'voyeur' in a far broader way than originally anticipated by either psychologists or the pornography industry. Film students are probably most familiar with notions of voyeurism through Laura Mulvey's famous 1975 essay "Visual Pleasure and Narrative Cinema."[46] Mulvey argued there are three types of voyeuristic gaze propelling the subjugation of women in mainstream cinema. First, there is the gaze of the camera surveying the scene, undetected by those it watches. Next, there is the editing, which tends to arrange narrative so that men are looking and women are being looked at. Finally, there is spectator, forced to identify with the look of the camera and editing and see as they see.[47]

Is the filmic gaze the webcam's gaze? Sometimes, it does seem that being a camgirl is similar to acting in your own movie or starring on your own reality television show. Yet there are at least four ways in which camgirls differ from film actresses or participants in reality TV. First, with few exceptions, camgirls are not subjected to directors or producers, but instead film themselves. Second, the Web's model of broadcasting is not one-to-many, as with film and television, but many-to-many. Certainly, viewers may choose to watch camgirls anonymously and silently, as if in a darkened, hushed cinema. However, they are by no means limited to this option. The homecam aesthetic supports a number of ways for viewers to interact with camgirls and one another, as we shall see. Third, the Web permits users to engage in simultaneous activities in ways impossible to imagine on film and television. A television chat-show host cannot talk to her producers, call her mother, and have an erotic encounter with her boyfriend while simultaneously taping her television show, but for many camgirls and viewers, multitasking is a way of life. Who is the object in these scenarios? Who is the subject?

The fourth difference between webcams, film, and television is that webcams are designed to broadcast their material live and unedited. Indeed, this is a huge part of their appeal. Whether fascinating or banal, all share a "fidelity to the moment," remarks Simon Firth.[48] As viewer Jason Thrice points out, this fidelity is linked to politics of representation:

> In the reality-television shows, they edit out the boring parts to package what's going to sell. But who makes that decision? Not the actors. Where in homecamming, they've got the direct power to turn off the cam, cover it up, reposition it or walk out of the room. I think that knowing the webcammer has the power to control what's presented actually makes me feel that what's happening on the cam is more real, less ... *contrived*.[49]

A number of critics (including Mulvey herself) have modified their position regarding film consumption and the male gaze since 1975. Today, most film theorists understand that sexuality, race, class, education, ability, and nationality may all alter spectators' identifications with the look of the camera, making it impossible to say what a viewing experience 'means' for every viewer. Yet as contested as it has become, Mulvey's theory of the gaze still explains much of the psychological power film has on viewers, even in the age of new media. Jason's comments about camera control, quoted above, recall a long history of feminist efforts to 'take back the gaze' in their avant-garde filmmaking practices.

The Aesthetics of the Grab

But on the Web, spectatorship functions less as gaze than grab. By 'grab,' I mean to clutch with the hand, to seize for a moment, to command attention, to touch—often inappropriately, sometimes reciprocally. To grab is to grasp, to snatch, to capture. Grabbing occurs over the Web in different ways during each stage of production, consumption, interpretation, and circulation.[50] With respect to production, the date and time stamp on most camgirl sites is an iconic reminder that webcams are generally set to take photos every few seconds or minutes, rather than continuously. With respect to consumption, camgirl viewership is more like partaking in a visual banquet than like grabbing something from McDonald's. Camgirls are viewed not on televisions but on crowded computer desktops that require viewers to click and drag between multiple windows and, of course, hide non-work-related images should a boss walk by. Given the reports that two-thirds of viewers go online at work at least once a day, this is not an uncommon scenario.[51]

To understand how the grab works with respect to homecam interpretation, one need only consider the expression 'screen grab.' Unlike film or television broadcasters, camgirls do not ordinarily archive the recurring images they put out into the world. Once a camgirl becomes popular, viewers often volunteer to set their computers to 'grab' images, but because there are no designated beginnings or endings to most camgirl performances, viewers feel no obligation to save every single screen grab downloaded. As a result, researchers at fan sites are often challenged to piece together what happened on a particular night in a camgirl's life by stitching together various viewers' selected shots that may or may not represent the entirety of the evening's events.

Finally, the grab is at play in the process of circulation, for once an image begins to travel around the Web, it is impossible to control where it will wind up. At the exact moment a camgirl is broadcasting, fans and critics are creating their own Web pages that laud or mock the 'reality' they see on their screens, and using screen grabs to make their point. Although copyright protects a camgirl to some degree, fair use and parody place her at the mercy of the viewers, putting her very identity up for grabs. In the time it would take to call a lawyer, viewers have taken a camgirl's image and reused it, often making community with one another, sometimes becoming microcelebrities themselves in the process.

Grabbing at Commodity

Rather than considering it the newest form of voyeurism, the grab is better understood through the mechanics of "commodity fetishism," a term coined by Karl Marx.[52]

"A fetish is an object masquerading as a story," psychiatrist Robert Stoller once wrote.[53] The word 'fetish' was invented by anthropologists, who were astonished when they discovered Africans not only accepted, but invested spiritual energy in, the cheap beads they were offered from European traders in return for valuable items like spices and furs. Marx found the "mist-enveloped regions of the religious world" the perfect setting for his analysis of commodity fetishism, a European version of the African's "savage delusion."[54]

Like anthropologists in Africa, Marx was astonished by the way modern consumers invested psychic energy in goods that in no way reflected the labor put into them. Put in economic terms, commodity fetishism describes what happens when exchange value trumps use value in an open marketplace.

As any woman who has ever hungered for a Manolo Blahnik shoe after watching Sarah Jessica Parker in *Sex and the City* can attest, brands and celebrities are classic commodity fetishes. In the postmodern moment, both brand and contemporary celebrity draw their power not from any sort of utility, but rather from their ability to serve as social identifiers. It is important to understand that this identification is hardly unidirectional: New Yorkers mock women in 'Carrie Bradshaw shoes' as often as they admire them.

Camgirls—who combine branding and celebrity on their own terms—are likewise taken up or rejected by viewers as commodity fetishes. It is common to see webcam viewers behaving as brand loyalists fighting for what they want in a particular camgirl, rather than switching to a new one. It is also true that viewer input often causes camgirls to alter their behavior online in such a way that a site that began as a life cam slowly morphs into an art cam, or a site that began as an art cam morphs into a porn cam, and so on. I realized this the day I found the webcam of New York "crackpot sexologist" Ducky Doolittle.[55] Knowing Ducky was a former pinup girl, I was expecting to see something more glamorous than a topless woman typing to viewers while wearing clown makeup. I quickly learned that Ducky's definition of glamour (and sex, and fame, and community) was utterly her own. "I used to not interact with my fans much," Ducky confessed. "I though the bulk of them were adult magazine perverts who had no sincere interest in me." She continued:

Figure 9. Ducky Doolittle. Courtesy Ducky Doolittle.

But after opening up my chat room I have found out that I have a lot more female fans. And that my fans are much cooler and more intelligent than I ever imaged. I've fallen in love with them. Some nights I am the only pervert in my chat room! They are all talking about corn dogs and clowns! I chat every Sunday night and I'd say half the conversation is about clowns. They are so funny![56]

When Brands Fail to Please: The Case of Vera Little

Not all viewer interactions go as smoothly as the ones Ducky describes. In fact, it is usually only a matter of time before a camgirl's viewers realize that despite her packaging, she is not a brand to be consumed, but rather a human being engaged in a particular type of labor. In the film *Live Nude Girls Unite*, a stripper's client asks, "What's your job?" To which she replies, "I am a stripper." The client's response is to qualify the question: "I mean," he says, "how do you earn a living?"[57] A similar disavowal occurs in camgirl communities.

"People are half right—setting up a cam *is* easy, and that's why everyone thinks they can do it," explains former AnaCam webmaster Jason Shapiro. "It's another thing when they try to offer content for it. … Typically they burn out after a few months when they realize that sustaining a creative edge to the cam isn't all that easy, or instantly financially rewarding."[58]

An exemplary tale in this vein was narrated to me by Vera Little, a Canadian art student who began homecamming after a saline breast implant complication wound up leaving her a leg and finger amputee.[59] "The Vera Little Media Project is where I started to have webcam shows, and was an important step in learning to deal with my body image," Vera told me.[60] She described herself as playing a character online who served as her "super hero double":

[She has] unquestionable confidence, wit, always sporting a fashionable hair-do and ready for any social occasion. But she has a sense of humor and knows not to take herself very seriously. She's some combination of infallible super hero, tragic movie starlet, and ridiculous Price is Right girl all rolled up in one. In one hand she's holding a death ray gun, in the other a Jell-O mold.

In the past, Little had worked as a stripper and readily admits that her early webcam performances were designed to "give me the attention I craved from my work as a stripper (pre-amputee) but with the ultimate power of control through self-editing."

Yet after a year of camgirl shows, she felt what she calls "a familiar pull" in two directions. Little divides her audiences into two camps, based on the emails she receives and the sites that link to hers. The vast majority she describes as "hey, look at this weird site" visitors. "They tend to be under the age of thirty, often artists," she explains. "Many of them see amputation as an extreme example of body modification along the lines of tattoos, scarring, and piercing." For these individuals, Little works as a brand: in consuming her site, they are able to self-identify as part of a counterculture movement.

There is also a small contingent of viewers Little describes as "older, mostly married who are, for the most part, amputee devotees." In the language of sexology, these individuals are paraphiliacs or sexual fetishists: people erotically fixated on a specific, nongenital part of the body. As Little puts it: "They are really turned on by stumps."

Initially, it did not bother Little that she was expected to negotiate between those who wanted to consume her as a branded object and those who were consuming her as a sexual one. "I don't have any big issue with the sex industry," she explained, "and to some degree I still am a worker in that industry." Yet over time, it became clear that it was the sexual fetishists rather than the 'hip' users who were the ones defraying Little's bandwidth costs by becoming members at twenty dollars per month. Predictably, explains Little, "those members were way more interested in seeing me masturbate than wanting to watch something artsy. Shows like Stump Theater, where I dressed up my stumps and had a puppet show, were not box office successes, though they were among my personal favorites."

In the Introduction to this book, I suggested that camgirls work as emotional laborers, responsible for managing their feelings of others either through surface acting, or through deep acting, in which the employee truly identifies with the feelings needed to keep customers satisfied.[27] Although Little remembers feeling that she didn't want her site to "fall into just porn, which wasn't the original idea," she admits that it wasn't just the sexual fetishists who were starting to wear on her. Even when it came to servicing the hipster crowd, Little recalls, "I was beginning to feel burnt out playing for the cameras."

Off-camera, Little was working on sculpture and animation, things she felt would be of little interest to her present viewers. "I wanted the webcam to document more of the realities of my art making than to keep propagating a persona that I needed less and less," she explained. After careful consideration, Little created her Homunculus site, which she describes as a "portfolio of my work and the process of making it."[61]

As a brand, the Homunculus site is clearly less lucrative than the Vera Little Media Project. Certainly Homunculus gets less traffic than her original site. Although she still uses the name Vera Little ("for a number of reasons, mostly protection and for consistency") on Homunculus, both the super-vixen and the super-heroine roles appear to have fallen by the wayside. "[On Homunculus] my being an amputee has much more of a realistic role," explains Little. "[There, it's a] physical state that forces me to be more creative about the way I use tools and make art." For Little, though, the payoff in personal integrity has been worth the price of diminished branding power over the Web.

In his examination of the emotional labor of call center workers, Gavin Poynter found that when they perceived their customers as their equal, workers thought their emotional labor was an expression of their identity and thus a "good thing."[62] When they saw themselves as unequal, they viewed their emotional labor as a commodification of the self and thus a "bad thing." Poynter noted that these perceptions were not simple matters of choice, but depended on how the workers' labor was structured within specific economic settings. Whereas professional emotional laborers (such as freelance workers and distance educators) have "real discretion over ... their hours of work, their interactions with clients and customers and the nature of those interactions," nonprofessionals (Poynter mentions checkout operators, waiters, hotel staff, and call center employees) work under conditions that "assume their subservience" to both the employer and the customer. [63]

The Case of the Blogging Nanny

Yet in a networked world, the space between professional and nonprofessional emotional labor overlaps in confounding ways. In a July 2005 *New York Times* article, Helaine Olen confessed that as a forty-year-old mother of two, she felt "hip by proxy" to learn that her twenty-six-year-old nanny was keeping a blog.[64] However, when the nanny referred to her job as work in a "seemingly sarcastic fashion," explains Olen, "she broke the covenant":

> Most parents don't like to think the person watching their children is there for a salary. We often build up a mythology of friendship with our nannies, pretending the nanny admires us and loves our children so much that she would continue to visit even without pay.

With a single mention of emotional labor as "work," Olen admits that her nanny's blog went from a commodity capable of helping Olen feel young to a writ of judgment passed on her life by a difficult "do-me feminist with an academic bent." After Olen came upon a blog post in which the nanny contemplated sterilizing herself in reaction to a bad working week, she asked her husband to fire her.

The day Olen's story appeared in the press, the Web was full of links to the blog of "Tassy," the unnamed nanny in the article.[65] Hardly a voiceless migrant laborer, Tassy explained in her blog that she was working as a nanny to save money for graduate school. Countering Olen's worry that she might look at her life and find it wanting, Tassy noted that the only time she thought about her boss was in relation to her employment. "Would she manage her schedule so she would stop changing my hours?" asked Tassy. "Would she and her husband figure out if they were staying in Brooklyn so I would stop having to listen to them debate moving to the suburbs?" After conceding that "it was very naïve and foolish of me to have shown Ms. Olen my blog" and promising to blog anonymously from that point forward, Tassy urged people to discuss the "real issues at hand," such as "public utility and discourse about female sexuality, intergenerational sexism, ethical standards for national newspapers, prudent yet honest writing, and new spaces of discourse and their impact on privacy."

Olen's article and Tassy's blogged response show not only the impossibility of sustaining the fantasy of human as commodity (whether the commodity is called 'my camgirl,' or 'my nanny') but also how blurry Poynter's distinctions between professional and nonprofessional emotional labor become in the age of networks. When we read Tassy's words, to which person should we respond: the professional student who speaks about literature, the semiprofessional writer who works at keeping her blog audiences enlightened and entertained, or the nonprofessional nanny expected silently to mirror the demands of her client?

Toward a Strategic Essentialism

Questions like those above call to mind Gayatri Spivak's argument that terms such as 'woman,' 'black,' and 'Third World' are first and foremost a result of what others think of us, rather than what we think of ourselves.[66] This is because identity is never entirely self-derived, but results from 'grabs' as it circulates around the various networks through which we associate: our family, friends, employers, legal and medical systems, economies, nationalities, and so on.

Rather than embracing universality (the 'people are people' response) or resisting labels altogether (a gesture she sees as politically futile), Spivak urges a practice she calls "strategic essentialism." In strategic essentialism, individuals create new names for themselves that simultaneously generate feelings of affinity and contestation, as a form of catachresis.[67] The term 'women of color,' for example, simultaneously embraces a number of possible political alliances among radically different people, yet it also deliberately provokes the question of what we even *mean* when we say this.

Strategic essentialism holds that no label can ever fully describe who we are, yet urges people to position catachrestic identity as a way to build coalitions. Originally, Donna Haraway imagined that the cyborg would work this way, inspiring citizens to forge 'cyborg politics' based on new ideas of affinity in networks while continually asking themselves, "Who is the cyborg, anyway?" Perhaps more significant than Haraway's cyborg metaphor was her argument that First World and Third World women were connected through 'integrated circuits' of labor and consumption. A decade before anyone outside the academy knew the word 'globalization,' Haraway was urging feminists to analyze the currents of transnational networks connecting women around the world.

In 1984, Haraway scandalized the movement by arguing that she would rather be a cyborg than a goddess. Yet today, I think the metaphor of the camgirl does a better job. When I ask viewers why homecamming is such a female-dominated millieu, I often get the reply "That's just the way it is." Feminist labor theorist Laura Augustin describes a similar response when she asks why migrant women are employed in caretaking positions (migrant men are frequently employed as gardeners and mechanics.) She describes a belief that "across cultures, women [and not men] are those who 'know how' to care."[68]

Of course, this belief is as illogical (and as self-serving) as the notion that nimble fingers work best in sweatshop labor. It is a story about the nature of women designed to support the structural inequities of global economics. I am not saying that because camgirls share affinities with migrant female service workers (whom we might think of as 'forgotten cyborgs') these two groups are equivalent. Clearly, they are not. Yet a comparison of the two as emotional laborers reveals patterns that structure a great deal of women's emotional work around the globe.

Similar to camgirls, migrant women in caretaking positions are often dismissed as doing nothing, when clearly they are doing *something*. Similar to camgirls, these forgotten cyborgs hardly ever figure in political conversations, unless the subject is pornography, prostitution, or the sexual display of children. We may all be cyborgs now, but no woman thinks of herself as "just a camgirl," just as no service worker thinks of herself as simply a nanny, maid, exotic dancer, or home companion. All women rightly counter, "There is so much more to me than that!" It is feminism's job to ensure that every woman's "so much more" makes it into the conversation.

3. Being and Acting Online: From Telepresence to Tele-ethicality

"Do you think she'll show up in clown makeup?"
Stacy Pershall and I were in Ana Voog's New York City hotel room, musing about local camgirl Ducky Doolittle, the self-described "crackpot clown sexologist."[1] The three of us had gone to see a Laurie Anderson concert together, and we'd invited Ducky to have a drink with us after the show. While we waited, we speculated about how Ducky would come across in person.

"Maybe she'll sit on a cake. She's famous for that!" squeaked Ana.

A wail from the bed reminded us that before we could relax with Ducky, we needed to deal with the fact that Ana—who had attended the show wearing white dreadlocks and a fuzzy pink hood—had brought back a new friend "to talk." At first, the woman seemed intriguing enough: like us, she was a fan of Anderson; unlike us, she was apparently an avant-garde opera composer. But by the time we reached the hotel, we were throwing one another apprehensive glances. Our new friend had gone from chatty to silent to sullen inside the space of twenty minutes. Now—as she lay on the bed, warbling what appeared to be original compositions to the hotel ceiling—we realized that inviting her to the room had been a mistake.

As we debated strategies for dealing with Opera Woman, there was a knock. Ducky, sans clown makeup and looking every inch an ordinary New Yorker in a black jacket and leggings, walked in. As if in welcome, our friend reached a terrifying crescendo. Ducky immediately dashed from the room, explaining, "I forgot something in the lobby!"

A moment later, the hotel room phone rang. "It's the front desk," Ana told us. "The room next door is complaining about the singing and they say everyone without a reservation needs to leave our room immediately or they are calling the police."

The mention of the police roused Opera Woman from her fugue state. With some assistance, she was able to get to the elevator. I was about to leave the hotel room myself when Ducky returned. Surprised, I began explaining that we had to leave. "Ducky, I feel awful about this, but the hotel management says anyone in our room without a reservation ..."

"The management?" Ducky repeated, raising an eyebrow. "Terri, I went downstairs and made that call on my cell phone. When you grow up a homeless teenager, you learn to spot crazy people a mile away."

To me, this story is about the significance of presence. Like many Internet researchers, I don't believe that offline meetings are more real than reading someone's diary online, chatting over the Internet, or watching a webcam. In fact, I'm at times drawn to the opposite argument—that in some cases online meetings provide us with a *more* real experience of a person than a face-to-face encounter. Still, there is a reason that perfume scents are called essences, and when trying to express an elemental facet of someone's character, we often cite embodied details such as how they sound, smell, or move. I try to resist the admittedly seductive notion that I know 'the real camgirl' or viewer by dint of having spent time with her or him in person. Sociologist Erving Goffman once observed that we all have backstage and onstage manifestations of ourselves; camgirls who think of me as "that woman writing a book on homecamming" treat me differently than they do their longtime (backstage) friends, even if they extend themselves socially for me onstage. I find this behavior entirely appropriate.[2]

Nevertheless, each time I meet a camgirl or viewer in the flesh, I am reminded of that old Mark Twain saying, "You learn something swinging a cat by the tail you can learn no other way." I knew about Ducky's past, and perhaps could have deduced from her journal that she would be the type of person who could spirit a crazy person out of a hotel room with a minimum of fuss. The difference between knowing that about Ducky and experiencing it, however, is the difference between reading about water and going swimming. Live presence feels essential in a way that Web-based experiences do not—at least not yet.

In the last chapter, I urged feminists toward a strategic essentialism: a commitment to identity that nonetheless acknowledges all identities to be inaccurate and/or incomplete. Next, I want to take a closer look at how network society impacts what Spivak has called "the risk of essence," focusing especially on telepresence: the media-enabled feeling of 'really being there' with someone else, over a physical distance. I argue that rather than worrying about epistemology—"How can I know this experience is true?"—feminists need to emphasize the question of their responsibilities to the people they encounter online. I've dubbed this shift 'tele-ethicality': a commitment to engage, rather than forestall action in our mediated communities, despite the potential for fakery and fraud.

Online and Offline, Backstage and Onstage

Meeting camgirls and their viewers in the flesh has become a hobby of mine. Some come across as absolutely consistent with their online personas. Punk-rock-loving Stacy Pershall's piercings are outnumbered only by her tattoos, and in person, she looks like she just walked out of an underground show at a club you've never heard of. Ana Voog was in full 'fairie queen' regalia when we first met, long white dreadlocks falling on layer upon layer of diaphanous clothing. But even when appearance matches expectations, there are surprises—I never would have predicted Ana's rushed and breathy Minnesotan voice or her constantly fluttering hands. "Really, some people imagine me as … I don't even know what," Ana once told me, wide-eyed. "But if I had to describe myself, I'd say I am more like a Chihuahua than anything else." A Chihuahua from the cast of *Fargo*, perhaps.

Other people didn't match my expectations at all. Given online pornographer Danni Ashe's line of work, I expected her to show up at the SXSW New Media Conference in something racy: a pushup bra, high heels, maybe something in leather. Instead she wore a blue Oxford shirt and what my mother used to call "slacks." To the initial dismay of the room, Ashe's talk that day wasn't about male fantasy, but about combating online credit card fraud, a significant problem for the online porn industry. Danni is a magnetic presence, though, and before long the geeky audience began debating software protection with the same enthusiasm they would have shown had she given them a lap dance.

There are some subjects I've never gotten to meet in the flesh, and I often worry that my sense of their character suffers as a result. I was scheduled to speak on a panel with Jennifer Ringley in 2001, but after she backed out, I resigned myself to the fact that she would be my camgirl Godot.

I never go to meet a subject face to face these days without bringing a video camera or a tape recorder, and I increasingly find the technology shapes my interactions with them. When I look at a subject, I imagine the two of us in a camera's long shot. When I listen to her, I hear our conversation as a soundtrack—her voice, my voice, the sounds of a conference swirling around us, music in the background, even the music I might add if I were making our interview into a film. Barely at the level of consciousness, my brain keeps a running back channel of side notes, remarks, and links to check up on when we finish speaking, as if I were on the Web at that moment but lacked the electricity to follow my impulses.

Knowing that the camera, recorder, and even the Web will do the heavy lifting of full recollection for me allows me to give my live attention to random elements of my subjects' presentation that appear essential in some way. It could be the residual trace of her native Arkansas in Stacy's accent, or the scent of Lisa Batey's perfume (called "Happy," by the way). I suppose my hope is that these weird memory traces might work for me as they once did for Proust—details that recall the whole, the truth of it all, including the parts that the camera is missing. Why? What is it I am trying to capture?

"Even the most perfect reproduction of a work of art is lacking in one element: its presence in time and space, its unique existence at the place where it happens to be," wrote Walter Benjamin.[3] This presence, which Benjamin called "aura," helps explain my desire to meet my subjects live at least once, even though I encounter nearly all of them every day online. Yet to understand my desire to think of my live meetings as technologically mediated events, it is helpful to turn away from aura toward what theater critic Phil Auslander calls "mediatization."[4]

Today, we rely on technologies such as video cameras and microphones in two ways: The first is to help us remember events from the past. This is what instant replay technologies, photo archives, and recordings of concerts are for. The second is as means to more fully experience ourselves as live bodies existing in the present moment. Examples include the near-mandatory use of body mikes in live concerts, the ubiquitous screens around us that flash information such as time, temperature, and national debt, and the incorporation of PowerPoint technology into nearly every large university lecture hall. Camgirls and their viewers use technologies such as webcams and blogs in this second way, delivering a 'more real' version of their realities to one another by way of telepresence.

The Art and Science of Telepresence

Today, research on telepresence is being conducted in a number of fields, including communication, psychology, cognitive science, computer science, engineering, philosophy, and the arts. In their exhaustive review of literature on the topic, Teresa Ditton and Matthew Lombard isolate six main ways in which the experience of telepresence manifests itself: as realism (in the sense both of perceptual realism and of social realism), as a notion of "social richness," as the feeling of "transportation" (alternately, "you are there," "it is here," and "we are here, together"), as the quality of participatory immersion, as a belief that technologies function as a social actor within a medium, and, finally, as the perception that technology itself is a type of social actor.[5] Since all of these categories manifest themselves in homecamming to some degree, I want to consider each in detail.

Telepresence as Perceptual Realism

Ditton and Lombard define perceptual realism as "the degree to which a medium can produce seemingly accurate representations ... that look, sound, and/or feel like the 'real' thing."[6] In Chapter One, I described the way camgirls affect theatrical authenticity through image resolution. Resolution presents a paradox for those of us studying perceptual reality and the Web. Just as a carefully made-up woman can sometimes appear more 'natural' than her makeup-free counterpart, camgirls with better equipment, lighting, and more forethought present more vivid images. Viewers often unconsciously associate this clarity with reality, and often perceive seasoned camgirls as more natural than their plug-and-play counterparts.

Lighting significantly affects perceptual realism. Although I knew I wasn't coming across on the Web the way I looked in the mirror, I loved how the lighting in my room caused my webcam to read my dark brown hair as slightly blue. I might have found this unacceptable had I been an experienced photographer used to the light meters included in video and digital still cameras, designed to create good images even at low pixel resolutions. Like many camgirls, I began webcamming assuming that the only things I needed were minimal front lighting and a smile. I was wrong, but ignorance about lighting can bring about happy accidents such as blue hair.

This discussion has been proceeding on the assumption that the aim of every camgirl is to look her film starlet best, which is certainly not the case. When I first requested an interview with Auriea Harvey, an American artist who webcams from her home in Belgium, she refused me. "I am very interested in what you are doing," she wrote me, "I just don't feel comfortable defining beauty in this way." Auriea's answer confused me because she *is* quite conventionally beautiful, as her photos often demonstrate. Yet when I pressed for more information, Auriea explained that her webcam aesthetic differed from those of many other women online. "I never considered myself a camgirl," she told me, "because camgirls seem to make their webcams about themselves in a very surface kind of way, about sexuality and appearing 'beautiful.'" On the contrary, she explained, "My webcam is just on. It points at me when I am sitting at my desk working."[7]

Auriea might be surprised to learn that she has much in common with Kristie Alshaibi (known online as ArtVamp), an attractive, petite blonde art student with significant experience as a filmmaker. With her sense of drama and overcharged libido, Kristie ran a site that was quite popular, yet she was initially uncomfortable webcamming because she had difficulty letting the camera just be on, as Auriea puts it. Kristie explained to me how she eventually overcame her anxieties:

> The first time I saw my image on cam I immediately had to blur the camera and make it black and white. I took three shots and typed "last performance" on the picture to make it seem like I did that stuff all the time. ... I could not deal with myself in full focus, full color, going out to the world unedited. ... Finally I decided that if I were going to do this cam thing, I'd have to get over the issue of carefully controlling every image. It ran contrary to the nature of web cams. So

I did one more highly posed performance, only this time focusing on my every fault. I called the show "imperfection." And it broke open a whole new world for me.[8]

Telepresence as Social Realism

Kristie's concern that controlling images runs "contrary to the nature of webcams" is termed "social realism" by telepresence researchers. Social realism—which I take to be synonymous with theatrical realism—is "the extent to which a media portrayal is plausible or 'true to life' in that it reflects events that do or could occur in the nonmediated world."[9] The distinction between perceptual realism and social realism is significant. A science fiction story may not be perceptually realistic, but it may be socially realistic if it contains believable characters. In contrast, webcam viewer Howie notes that reality entertainment shows often contain high levels of perceptual realism, yet still come across as socially unrealistic. "*Survivor* is too different from real stranded people," Howie points out. "There is no panic to get rescued. *Gilligan's Island* was more real."[10]

In deference to the codes of social realism, I tried to be as natural on my webcam as possible, and, like many other camgirls, I often forgot the camera was there. I should also point out that mine was not a full-time, 24/7 webcam, and when I left the house for long periods of time, I turned my computer off, rather than keeping my webcam focused on an empty chair. Before I did, though, I went through something of a ritual in which my need for social realism battled my personal vanity. When I was sitting in front of a camera that refreshed every twenty seconds, I accepted whichever shot of me wound up on the Web. But if I was going to leave one static picture of myself up for a few hours (or days, when I went on vacation) I waited for a shot that was flattering, and left that one up as my final frame.

"Wow," camgirl Lisa Batey mused when I told her about my negotiations with myself. "I guess I just don't get all that introspective about the camera." When I met her in 2001, Lisa had already been homecamming for four years.[11] The jealous part of me would like to believe Lisa was lying about her lack of vanity, given the fact that she has been blessed with high cheekbones, wide eyes, and a trim body. But I've spent enough time with her in person to know she was telling the truth, and that as glamorous as she might appear, she's very much a tomboy at heart. As a friend of mine once said, "For someone who looks like a fashion model in still pictures, Lisa allows herself to look more hideous on her webcam than anyone I know. It's like she really is just living her life on the camera."

For months after talking to Lisa, I thought I was the only camgirl to be so utterly vacuous as to arrange my webcam shots from time to time.

One day, however, I was chatting online with Maura of Maura.com, and I blurted out my confession. In my mind, I could almost see Maura simultaneously pushing her glasses up her nose with one hand and twisting her curly hair in the other, baffled that I was so traumatized. "My God," she messaged me:

> There's even a term for that. It's called staging the parting shot. Believe me, if you are the kind of person who blows off your homecam for weeks at a time, like me, you get really good at parting shots. In fact, I think it might be what I like best about this webcam stuff. It's funny. I feel far more obligated to be raw and real in my online writing than I do on the camera.[12]

Telepresence as Intimacy and Immediacy

Maura's comments about feeling more obligated to be real in her online writing than on her camera speak to a notion that telepresence researchers call "social richness." Intimacy is one hallmark of social richness; immediacy (discussed next) is the other. Maura finds online writing to be more intimate than webcamming, in part because she is a longtime member of the blogging subculture. But for every person who feels writing to be more intimate than image, there is another who feels the opposite. Cam viewer Scott Ecksel, a teacher and fiction writer from Washington D.C., describes the intimacy he felt once after watching Ana Voog on her webcam. "At first," he recalls, "I was just hoping she'd masturbate." But then something happened:

> I was watching her watch the movie "The Green Mile." ... At the end of the movie, she had tears running down her cheeks. I don't know how to describe it; it was just utterly moving watching her emotion. It also felt uncomfortable, particularly in light of my original reason for wanting to watch her. I felt that a sort of violation was going on, that I was seeing something I had no right whatsoever to be seeing ...[13]

Although I don't mean to diminish the experience Scott relates, it is important to note that Ana Voog herself feels differently about the question of violation. Indeed, if Voog has one crusade, it is to convince her viewers that because what they are seeing reflects their feelings, rather than her own, violation via webcam viewership is impossible. Alan, a longtime viewer, describes his experiences watching the AnaCam:

> Something odd happens to me while watching AnaCam. Without traditional dramatic development, I automatically search for metaphors and imagine motivations. Ana's space lends itself to this by providing novel props, pets, and general clutter.

Then the scene updates. The new frame is the now moment. Real. The metaphors and imagined motivations detach from the moment. They are inspired, but not created, by Ana. Owning this stuff made me uncomfortable at first. Then, the experience quickly became entertaining and enlightening. Ana knows that viewers project themselves onto her website. She facilitates it. She has control over what the viewer sees and is competent at using that control. I also have control. If the site is boring, I can mouse click to something else without making excuses or hurting feelings.[14]

In his description of "the now moment," Alan invokes a notion that telepresence researchers call "immediacy." A moment possesses immediacy when there is no editing process to come between the viewer and the viewed—when the viewer has the sensation of experiencing events as and how they happen.

Telepresence as Transportation

Three distinct transportation metaphors are commonly used in descriptions of presence, argue Ditton and Lombard. The first is "you are there," in which the user is transported to another place. The next is "it is here," in which another place and the objects within it are transported to the user. Finally, there is "we are together," in which two (or more) communicators are transported together to a place that they share.[15] "You are there" is the oldest form of telepresence, going back as far as oral storytelling traditions. When readers speak of being transported by a narrative, they are articulating this model of telepresence, which explains why, for many, online diaries offer the most compelling sense of who a camgirl 'really' is. As writer and homecam viewer Ira from Texas puts it, "Every [diary] I read feels like another door opening in my head."[16]

The "it is here" model reverses the "you are there" equation. Quoting a famous study on television-watching processes, Ditton and Lombard note how some viewers felt "not so much that [they] are being taken out into the world, as that the world is being brought to [them]."[17] For the camgirl, Ditton and Lombard's "it is here" sense of telepresence may encompass the feeling that her viewers "are here" in her space.

The shared space, "we are together," version of telepresence seems in some ways an obvious model for an intimate, often interactive medium like the webcam. But it is a conceptualization of the camgirl-viewer relationship that most camgirls adamantly reject. Viewers who expect one-on-one interaction with camgirls learn early on, for instance, that asking a camgirl to wave for them is the quickest way to get told off. A camgirl may seem to be in a viewer's space, or vice versa, but acknowledging that sharing of space erases a boundary that few camgirls are willing to relinquish.

Telepresence as Sensory Immersion

Many people (in particular, virtual reality researchers) hold fast to the notion that the more the senses are engaged in a display of media presence, the more involved end users feel themselves to be.[18] This notion of sensory immersion explains the interest in homecamming technologies that bring sound and full-motion video to the viewing public. As Marcellus, a longtime viewer of the JenniCam, put it, "When Jenni [experimented briefly with] streaming, we got an even closer look at her." Echoing Marcellus, Artvamp sometimes regrets not using streaming on her site. "I wouldn't have been been able to fake anything," she explains:

> With sound I can't talk to one friend on the phone and say one thing and then talk to someone else and change my story. I'll be found out. ... This is wonderful [because it] forces complete honesty, and I am all for that. Complete lack of pretension was one of my goals in doing this. ... Because what we say is often more subject of rumor and innuendo than an image of us on the screen, the addition of sound complicates matters, and I love that kind of complexity.[19]

And yet such a positive view of streaming is hardly universal. Several camgirls began their webcams with streaming technologies but soon abandoned them. "I only had streaming video and audio briefly, and I really disliked it very much," Jennifer Ringley told me.[20] Andrea Mignolo, who was streaming from HereandNow, told me, "I did not talk to the cams. I couldn't. I'll sit on cam in front of my machines all day, and happily go about my business, but talking to the cams just doesn't happen."[21]

Telepresence as Psychological Immersion

A related phenomenon to sensory immersion is what Ditton and Lombard call "psychological immersion."[22] When people speak of a technology being 'addictive,' what they really mean is that it is highly immersive, so much so that it cuts into other activities in their lives. The kinds of interpersonal engagement that online technologies make possible can be extremely immersive even when sensory stimuli are impoverished—consider the reader of a comments thread who compulsively refreshes the page to keep the conversation going, or the web surfer who loses all sense of time while following a meandering trail of hyperlinks.

As the allusions to addiction indicate, psychological immersion is sometimes a difficult experience to keep in balance with one's other commitments. When I asked viewers to describe their engagement in homecamming communities on a scale of one to ten, many echoed the feelings of viewer William: "My wife would say I am at 10, but I'd say somewhere around a 7."[23] Some camgirl viewers struggle to set and maintain limits on their involvement with online activities, and others hop between different forms of immersion online, leaving one when they begin to feel too sucked in.

Telepresence as an Actor

For some camgirls, webcams themelves function as what Ditton and Lombard call a "social actor" in their lives.[24] Viewer Ira once compared camgirls Ana Voog and Stacy Pershall by explaining, "Stacy wants the cams more, but Ana wants more cams. ... I expect new and bigger things at Ana, but I am happy for Stacy as she grows."[25] When I told Stacy about Ira's observation that she "wants the cams more," her response was "Sometimes I feel like the cams want *me* more!" I've interviewed several camgirls who explain in one breath that "the cameras aren't a big deal, and I generally forget they are on," yet in the next confess that they feel exhausted by the constant pressure of the webcam's eye.

I can recall one morning early in my own webcamming career when I woke up late and ran out of my house with wild hair and unbrushed teeth to make an emergency bank deposit. On the street, I took no notice of the people, who probably looked at me strangely as I hurtled on my way. When I got home, though, I remember thinking, "I guess I better shower and look like a human before getting in front of the webcam." As a friend pointed out later, I wasn't really showering for my homecam viewers—I hardly had any at that point. I showered for the camera itself.

Forms of Viewer Identification

Viewers often surprise me with their identifications regarding camgirls. The literary critic Hans Robert Jauss broke identification into five subcategories: associative (being "of the people"), sympathetic (being "day to day"), admiring (being "of a distance"), cathartic, and ironic.[26]

Viewer Marcellus told me he thought of Jennifer Ringley "like a daughter or a little sister." When pushed to describe what he meant by this, he added, "She's young, slightly erratic, but well meaning. She takes on life with gusto and very definitely leads with her heart. She's still trying to figure out who she is and where she's going and I find that cute and endearing."[27] In Jauss's scheme, Marcellus can be thought of as having an associative identification with Jennifer, perceiving her not as someone to be admired from a distance, but rather as 'one of us.' As Marcellus put it, "I'd like to see where she is when she's forty or fifty and has had time to reflect on her life."

Like Marcellus, Melissa (known online as Banshee) admitted, "After all this time watching someone it's easy to think of someone on a webcam as someone you know."[28] Melissa identified with camgirl Ana Voog in a way Jauss might call "sympathetic," noting that checking Voog's camera had become for her. "Like calling a friend to see what's new." Melissa was so inspired by camgirls that she was considering her own homecam, with which she "aspire[d] to do great things." Magenta, a homecam viewer and an art student from Mississippi, likewise admitted, "the whole idea of home-camming does appeal to me, though I am not sure if I'd want to be a 'star.'" Now that Magenta has her own homecam site, perhaps her opinion will change.[29]

When Jennifer Ringley scandalized many of her viewers by running off with the boyfriend of fellow camgirl Courtney, some viewers found themselves drawn to her life as catharsis, much the way one would watch a Greek tragedy. "It's strange to care so much about a person you have never met in person," viewer Marcellus admitted. "I guess I just can't stand mean people, and I try to do my best to give another point of view and get people to lighten up a little."

Some viewers lose interest in camgirls who fall off their pedestals. Here is homecam viewer Amy C's explanation of her early days watching Ana Voog:

> I had about a month of high on Ana, all the while wondering what it was about watching another person's life that was so cool for me personally. In a way it's not a hard question but I still felt weird about it because it was as opposed to a real connection with someone. I was interested in Ana for the creative aspects, the "performance" pieces she would do in front of the camera, the way she made it obvious this was a creative new medium, as well as the day to day stuff—the way an artist lived her life.[30]

Amy's description of her 'honeymoon period' watching Ana is representative of Jauss's admiring stage of identification. Yet after five months of viewing, Amy began to reflect on her interest in the Anacam in a way that Jauss might term "ironic," confessing that it probably was no accident that her interest in Voog's camera mapped neatly to the fact that Amy's own life was "growing more complicated." We might also say that Ana Voog served as a cathartic idenfitication for Amy, in that Voog's "creative new medium" mirrored Amy's own attempts at personal growth during her most feverish period of spectatorship.

As Amy's story shows, not every viewer positively identifies with camgirls, and some spend copious amounts of time and energy creating Internet sites that mock them. It is interesting that some of the people who began these sites started as fans, but when a particular camgirl did something that displeased them (such as sleeping with another camgirl's boyfriend) their identifications turned to disavowal. If an unsuspecting fan had wandered into the Usenet group alt.fan.jennicam at the height of Ringley's fame in 2001, looking for like-minded viewers, she would have quickly discovered that the group had long since mutated into an online Mystery Science Theater for JenniCam haters. Those who identifed positively or even neutrally with Ringley were quickly advised to "get real" by community members, many of whom saw their constant surveillance of the JenniCam as a public service of sorts. Although the Jennicam shut down long ago, a similar 'love to hate' dynamic can be found on Encyclopedia Dramatica, a Wikipedia-inspired site devoted to mocking micro-celebrities on LiveJournal and elsewhere on the Web.[31]

The positive and negative identification scenarios I have sketched out here are extremes, and most viewers don't love or hate a particular camgirl. Instead, they evaluate camgirls against one another as brands and make judgments accordingly. For instance, viewer Alan calls Jennifer Ringley "a fairly ordinary girl, doing fairly ordinary things, in an extraordinary situation," confessing that he finds camgirl Ana Voog's "fractured grammar, transposed letters, cutesy lack of capitalization, gratuitous emoticons, and *that's way too much information* girl talk" more interesting by comparison.[32]

From Telepistemology to Tele-ethicality

Whatever forms they take, both telepresence and identification depend upon what philosopher Jacques Derrida would call "the metaphysics of presence": the conviction that somewhere beyond representation there exists essence, knowable and securable through the body.[33] Certainly, my desire to meet my Web-based subjects in the flesh is connected to this conviction. Of course, the increasing effectiveness of remote technologies (including satellites, robotics, and global media) makes it difficult to sustain belief in distinct categories of the here and the there, to say nothing of the virtual and the real. Computer scientist Ken Goldberg argues that the age of presence has been eclipsed by the time of telepistemology: the search for truth at a distance.[34] "Are we being deceived [by our media]?" asks Goldberg. "What can we know? What should we rely on as evidence?"[35]

Students of computing history will find the roots of Goldberg's telepistemology in the work of Alan Turing, the father of machine intelligence.[36] In the now-famous Turing Test, a human is placed in front of a computer terminal. She is told that she will be communicating online with two entities, one human and one machine. Using only their typed responses to her typed questions, the test-taker is asked to say which is the machine and which is the human, and further to determine the gender of the human.[37] In *How We Became Posthuman*, N. Katherine Hayles calls the Turing Test a magic trick. "The important intervention comes not when you try to determine which is the man, the woman, or the machine," she argues, "but when you willingly subject [yourself] to a cybernetic circuit whereby humanity is adjudicated solely through screen-based evidence." She explains, "As you gaze at the flickering signifiers scrolling down the computer screens, no matter what identifications you assign to the embodied entities that you cannot see, you have already become posthuman."[38]

According to Jodi Dean, telepistemology works its own posthuman magic. She points to the fact that, despite our increased ability to conduct research in pursuit of the truth, media-saturated publics are now locked into a "frightening silence, a kind of paralysis in which there are all sorts of plausible responses, all sorts of information available (out there, if we can find it)—but ultimately, nothing we can say."[39] As a means to combat this paralysis, I would urge what I call tele-ethicality: a commitment to engage, rather than forestall action in our mediated communities, despite the potential for fakery and fraud. To demonstrate what I mean, I relate the story of Karen.

Camgirl in Crisis

It was July. I had no air conditioner, which made working in my Brooklyn apartment impossible. I did, however, have a student ID and I knew that at New York University, the computer labs were always air-conditioned. I was working on my dissertation that summer and taking periodic breaks to skim LiveJournal, where I had made a number of online friendships. As I clicked through LiveJournal, I wound up at the blog of Karen and hesitated for a moment. Karen was one of the camgirls I was writing about, and though I had great fondness for her, I often found her behavior disturbing. An extremely compelling and charismatic personality, Karen spends a good portion of her life battling a bipolar disorder.

For someone who thinks about self-presentation in the public sphere, bipolarity is a fascinating disease. The older term for the illness is 'manic depression,' and, indeed, bipolar patients suffering manic episodes are often brilliant, articulate, and just plain fun. More than once, I expressed my concern to Karen that running a 24/7 webcam from her home might put her on the wrong side of people's unreasonable expectations and exacerbate her fight with bipolarity. She even confessed her frustration with viewer responses to her life that remained polarized between empty "You go girl" exhortations and "All you want is attention, you pathetic pig" condemnations. Still, she told me, to make her art, she needed to be utterly honest with her viewers, and she rejected the notion that those with mental illness had to live only as patients, as if they had no other facets to their identity.

Early during our time together, I told Karen that although I sympathized with her, I also needed to protect myself from her emotionally, so as not to relive some of the more horrible moments of my childhood. Karen was extremely gracious and understanding about my need for limited intimacy with her. Though I had her home phone number and address in town, she didn't pressure me to spend too much time with her, and I was grateful. I still kept tabs on Karen from a distance, however, because I am quite fond of her as a person. I knew from reading her journal that Karen had a therapist she trusted, and that she was taking medications to manage manic episodes. I had also read that Karen had been suffering a number of ups and downs related to finances and her love life lately and that she was concerned about her recent mood swings.

I knew that Karen's relationship had been on the rocks. She had written a few journal entries explaining that she was feeling unattractive and not worth having around. I wasn't shocked to read in her journal that her relationship had broken up, though I was sad that her lover had done the breaking up via email, rather than face to face. I knew Karen was hurting, but it was her second journal entry that day—posted just moments before I read it—that began to worry me: something to the effect that "it's no use anymore. My cat knows what is going to happen …" This was exactly the same language Karen had used a year earlier when she had tried to commit suicide in front of her webcams.

Not wanting to become overly involved in the situation, but nonetheless concerned, I decided to type in the URL for Karen's webcam site. "I am sure it's nothing," I remember thinking to myself. I was positive I'd see a picture of Karen on her bed, perhaps calling someone in tears. When you watch camgirls, that's a picture you get used to seeing.

Instead of tears, what I saw was Karen sprawled on her bathroom floor with three empty bottles of pills around her. As I mentioned, immediacy is a hallmark of webcamming, and my first concern was how long she had been lying there in that way. Assuming she took the pills after posting to her journal, I reasoned that she was probably within one or two minutes of overdosing. Karen's camera was on a twenty-second refresh, and the new image showed her curled up on the floor in almost a fetal position. Was that better or worse than the previous shot, I wondered? I thought that perhaps I should call 911, but then remembered that I didn't have Karen's address with me at school, so I wouldn't even know where to send the emergency medical services. Calling the police and giving them a URL wasn't going to do much good.

Community in Crisis

Frustrated, I went back to her LiveJournal, where I found others were having the same thoughts. I knew that many people listed Karen as a LiveJournal friend, and in the space of three minutes, I realized at least a dozen people had made comments urging her not to hurt herself and asking whether she needed help. Remembering just how popular her cam was, I consoled myself with the thought that someone would surely take control of the situation. Unfortunately, within minutes, it became clear that although Karen had a great many viewers, none of those who were online had her home address.

As hundreds, or possibly thousands, of viewers watched Karen die on her floor, I left the air conditioning of NYU and got on the subway back to my apartment and my address book. The subway ride took approximately thirty minutes, and I had plenty of time to think about what had happened. To my embarrassment, I realized that I was more irritated than anything else by this incident. It was unbearably humid, and I was under intense pressure to finish up the assignment I had been working on at school when this all began. Before I left school, I had wasted forty seconds of Karen's life capturing the images from her floor onto my hard drive. I was, after all, on a deadline for my book, and the images might help me think about it all later.

Realizing just how morbid I was being, I thought about how the word 'deadline' is so overused these days. I might have felt as if I was going to die from my dissertation, but the only person who was, in fact, dying was on the floor in her bathroom. I got off at my stop and headed to my apartment. I grabbed my address book and my computer mouse simultaneously. After I looked up Karen's address, I went to her journal site. By that time Karen had made another post, telling people to stop worrying about her.

Horrified that Karen appeared to have the fortitude to get to her computer journal but not to dial 911, I scrolled back through her journal comments. It turned out that while I was on the subway, a friend had remembered Karen's home phone number. Another person did some investigating on the Web and located Karen's address from her online résumé. Both individuals dialed 911. I read further and came across a post from Karen's boyfriend, the one she had presumably been thinking of when taking the pills. He wrote that he was on the phone with her, that there were EMS technicians at her door, and that she was sending them away. He was understandably shaken and was urging others to redial 911. I sat down on my bed to think. What was my responsibility here? I knew this person as a dissertation subject, not as a close friend. The authorities had been alerted, and Karen had dismissed them. I did not want to be involved in this. "Probably the EMS folks will come back," I thought. "Probably those who know Karen better than I do will stop over at her house in a minute. I'll see them on camera, and then I'll know I can stop worrying." I looked at her camera again, and Karen was still on the bathroom floor, this time cradling the telephone.

Suddenly, I had an idea. I would call Karen's number and leave a message on her answering machine. I knew she was talking on the phone, so I wouldn't have to speak with her. I'd get her voice mail. But she would know that I was worried about her—at least as worried as someone who leaves a voice message can be. "Well," I rationalized to myself, "A phone call uses my voice. That's more personal than leaving a note in her journal, right?" Busy rehearsing what I would say into her answering machine, I was caught off guard when she answered the phone. I did a lousy job of covering for myself, but Karen was far too doped up on medications to know that. I asked her how she was, and she told me she couldn't talk and that the police were there, but added that they were leaving her apartment soon and that she'd call me back. This didn't strike me as a good idea, and before I realized what I was doing I told her I was coming over to her house to talk. She said she would like that, and we hung up the phone.

On my third subway trip of the day, I started to pout in earnest. I thought about how many times in graduate school I'd argued that theory and practice were equally important. Hadn't today shown me that speaking about something and doing something are not equivalent, regardless of how performative language is? Sure, Karen had hundreds of "cyber hug" well-wishers on her online journal, most of whom were far less bitter and angry than I was. Yet I appeared to be the only one heading to her house to check on her drug overdose. Something was very wrong with this. I had more time to ponder the problems of the mediated life as I rang Karen's doorbell—three times—and waited for her to respond. As my body relaxed with each unanswered ring, it told me just how much I didn't want to deal with this situation. If I ring a doorbell and there is no answer, then nobody is home, right? And if nobody is home (or if they are ignoring the bell), I cannot be held responsible for her well-being, right?

"Nobody expects that of me," I thought, simultaneously wondering just who I thought "nobody" was. I was almost ready to turn around and get back on the train, rehearsing in my head what I would type on Karen's journal. "I talked to her on the phone, and I went over there, but nobody answered the bell, so I figured EMS had taken her for treatment, and I came home to check her webcam."

Just as I was about to leave, I remembered that Karen's doorbell had been broken the last time I had come to visit. Frustrated, I began pounding on her window. Her door opened, and I saw her husband (from whom she was separated) heading down the hallway to let me in. The two of us must have set off for her apartment at about the same time. He told me that Karen had been taken to the hospital after all. He had not arrived in time to see her go, but he had spoken to the nurses in the emergency room, who said that Karen was receiving activated charcoal for her overdose and was more or less fine. We spoke in the kitchen while the cameras continued to record our movements. For some reason, neither of us considered turning off the cameras. Only Karen could do that.

"You don't have to go there," I kept telling myself. Ever since I watched my mother die of brain cancer, I've hated hospitals, particularly emergency rooms. In an emergency room, privacy is impossible. To keep up with their large patient loads, overworked nurses are instructed to keep everyone within eyeshot. Giving privacy to patients makes that more or less impossible.

The moment I walked into the ER and saw the makeshift privacy curtain around Karen, I knew she wasn't "fine." Those curtains get pulled only when one patient is doing something so upsetting that it might compromise the care of the other patients around her. When I got behind her curtain, I saw why Karen had been hidden. Her body had decided to expel the charcoal it was being fed (quite common) and she had thrown up, over everything. Her bed sheets, her nightgown, her arms were all covered in charcoal. The floor around her bed looked as though someone had dropped a water balloon filled with ink. At the center of this scene Karen was spitting up and yelling for someone—anyone—to call her boss. Somehow she had remembered she was supposed to be at work. The nurses were trying to calm her down. I made the call to Karen's boss, who already knew what was happening (a friend from across the country was an avid viewer of Karen's cam). Karen and I spoke a little, and then she dozed. Occasionally she would have a seizure.

When Karen seized, her arms and legs shot straight in the air, her face went slack, and her entire torso convulsed. Her eyes rolled back in their sockets until no part of the iris was visible. For the person seizing, time has no meaning. For the person watching, each second is interminable. I waited each seizure out—there were four in the time I was there. Every one left Karen disoriented and bewildered. More than once she asked who I was and why she was there. If you've ever been asked that question you know how terrifying it can be, both for the person asking and for the person answering.

Later on, I ran into one of the EMS workers who had stopped by to see "his girl Karen." He asked whether I knew she had a camera in her bathroom, and I said yeah. He smiled and said, "It got me. Who knows? I might wind up on Rescue 911." I considered once again something I had been thinking about since that morning: would Karen have attempted suicide had her cameras not been broadcasting her attempt to reach her estranged boyfriend? Maybe taking the cameras down would be the only way to help this situation.

On the other hand, perhaps the issue wasn't that the cameras were broadcasting, but that there were too few of them. I can't imagine anyone romanticizing an overdose once they'd witnessed its violent effects on the body of a friend.

The MasterCard Parody

I left after about three hours. Karen was cleaned up and they were prepping to move her to a room. I was told that if I called the desk in the morning they'd tell me where she was.

I returned to my apartment and to my computer, where I saw that LiveJournal had been quite active in my absence. Karen's husband had posted on her journal that she was safely in the hospital, and thanked everyone for their concern. The owner of Karen's ISP had detailed how her site's viewership had spiked during her suicide attempt, and then dipped after the EMS unit had arrived. He had also voiced concern over who would foot the bandwidth bill. And in the true spirit of free speech on the Internet, someone was already circulating a parody of the day's events. One of Karen's webcammed images—a shot of her lying next to her toilet—had been juxtaposed with text in the style of a MasterCard commercial:

50–750 mg of [First Medication]	$42.87
75–200 mg tablets of [Second Medication]	$62.32
LiveJournal account	$15.00
4 webcams and a website	$500.00
Suicide attempt capturing the drama:	PRICELESS[40]

Neither the anger at the overdose nor its expression in the form of parody surprised me. Rage is a frequent, and understandable, response to a suicidal act, and appropriation through transgressive 'grab' is, as I have discussed, a common tactic for managing trauma in camgirl communities. By the time I returned from the hospital, though, the MasterCard post had eclipsed Karen's overdose as the main topic of discussion. Someone had suggested that LiveJournal should take the parody down, others had invoked the right to freedom of expression, and still others had claimed that the law was on Karen's side, and would forbid any images of Karen being used without her express consent. That night, as Karen lay seizing, people all over LiveJournal entertained themselves with the virtualities known as free speech and copyright law.

Although the parody didn't surprise me, I was shocked to learn that its creator was Cameo Davine, the very woman who had found Karen's address and called 911.[41] I went to Cameo's LiveJournal site to see whether she offered any explanation. In a post on her own journal she explained that she, like many of us, had been trying to contact Karen privately for weeks now, and had been ignored. She said that she had gotten in trouble at work for calling 911 when the police, suspicious of the call, had stopped by to see whether she was "for real." She explained how frustrated and helpless she had felt watching Karen on her bathroom floor, with enough wherewithal to post to LiveJournal but not enough to call for help. Her parody, Cameo argued, had been written in the hopes that it would wake Karen up to the fact that she needed far more help than she would admit.

Reading all this, I decided to comment in Cameo's journal. I wrote that I certainly didn't believe that her parody should be censored, and that Cameo should take note of the fact that Karen was now unconscious in the hospital, making 'wake-up calls' somewhat moot. I urged Cameo to take down the parody in the interest of compassion, and to write me personally if she wanted to talk further. Shortly after I posted, Cameo sent me an email requesting that I call her on the telephone. She also mailed me her newest LiveJournal post, which read, "this ... is not helping anyone, and it's hurting me. This sullies my reputation as a thinking, feeling, compassionate being into just another smart-ass. ... That is not what I am. So I am changing the presentation."[42]

That three-hour phone conversation with Cameo was the most exhausting and most gratifying virtual experience I've had in my life to date. Cameo discussed her feelings of helplessness, and I admitted I shared them. Talking about her parody, she confessed, "This was just something that came out of me. I didn't know it would get spread all over the Net like this, and now I feel like I am defending a piece of art—if I even want to call it that—which was made in about three minutes while enraged."

Cameo and I agreed that if she wanted to make more parodies but wasn't sure whether or not they were "ready for primetime," she was welcome to send them to me via email prior to posting. I told her I would evaluate them (as best I could) as political art objects. The next day I received an email with the words "you said I could" attached. Before my eyes flashed different photos of LiveJournal user icons, and words that read:

> 1000+ watched while Karen attempted suicide on her webcam for the second time.
> Only 2 calls were placed to 911.
> 1000+ messages of moral support were posted on Livejournal.com.
> 6 legal threats and 2 acts of censorship were made to threaten artists.
> 1 offer was made by a friend to pay post-mortem webcam fees.
> Only 1 Livejournal.com "friend" visits her in the hospital.
> 1 girl
> Attempted suicide
> Alone
> While the world watched.
> Guilty bystanders, focus on the good you can do.[43]

Taking the Risk of Essence

I am not the first person to note that time passes exceedingly quickly on the Internet. Over the next few weeks, Cameo was busy traveling for work, and the energy she had available for Karen was limited. She never posted the second project—until I reproduced it for this book, I was the only person who had seen it.

It took me a long time to decide to tell this story here, and I am still ambivalent about it. I may be telling it wrong, and it may be the wrong story to tell. Karen has seen what I have written, and I don't want to cause her any further discomfort or anxiety. For a time after her hospitalization, Karen made a decision to keep her cameras on, to show people how her struggle to be an artist in the face of a difficult childhood and a complex medical present shouldn't be hidden from public view, but shared. I've made a different, but in some ways related, decision, choosing to write my reaction to these events as publicly and as truthfully as I know how.

When we are online, many of us who would never think to abuse or ignore someone suffering in a face-to-face setting find ourselves caught in the seduction of the virtual. It is easy to forget that in network society, viewed and lived experiences aren't mutually exclusive categories. A well-traveled Netizen will run into a suicide threat nearly once a week, and it is easy to become inured. But does it make any sense to treat the online threat as less real than the one made from the rooftop?

Such questions are particularly pressing for those of us inhabiting women-dominated online spaces. Elizabeth Donaldson writes that historically, women's mental illness has lent itself more to virtualizing than other conditions. She notes that ever since *Jane Eyre* was published, feminist literary critics have celebrated women's madness in fiction as metaphorical transgression against patriarchy. Yet outside the realm of fiction, she argues, mentally disabled women have been left to fend for themselves, their narratives and needs dismissed as 'crazy.'[44] If women's mental illness is seen as virtual in offline space, how much more so must it be online?

I began this chapter by relating what I viewed as a testimony to live presence, discussing why I meet my book subjects face to face and explaining the way Ducky handily dismissed a 'crazy' woman from our hotel room. Even in that moment, I knew this women was less a threat than an inconvenient reminder of my past struggles with mental illness. (Obviously, Ducky may have perceived the situation differently.) I like to think of myself as a kind person, but that night I did not think kindness extended to keeping a mentally ill stranger in a friend's hotel room. Yet I did venture to Karen's side when she was in crisis, despite having distanced myself from her. Then, after I was sure Karen was safe, I spent time on LiveJournal talking to Cameo and others. Why?

"For every complex problem, there is a solution that is simple, neat, and wrong," wrote H. L. Mencken. The simplest explanation for why I went to Karen's home and her hospital bed is that I had met her in the flesh, we had socialized, and she was real to me. Yet I had also met Opera Woman, and I had done nothing.

The complex explanation for why I visited Karen has to do with my general reactions to telepresence and my specific relationship to the LiveJournal members who gathered on her site during her hospitalization. One of the reasons I am drawn to online communities is that in my physical world, I have a very strong fight-or-flight response that causes me to react more harshly to provocation than I would like. Rather than using online communities as venues for anonymity and antisocial behavior, I've long thought of them as life-training classrooms with both a built-in excuse to delay responses and a "paper trail." To paraphrase the poet Anne Sexton, my LiveJournal sees more than I, and remembers it better. Sexton used her radio to soothe and ground herself; I often find myself looking at old webcam shots or rereading posts in my LiveJournal to let the "music swim back to me."

In those moments of contemplation and reflection, I feel the space of tele-ethicality. I hear the voice that calls me to admit to myself that the Karen who touched me with her writing on the Web is just as real to me as the woman who frightens me on the bathroom floor. I understand that life is not television, and if I can help, I should. I can stop my fetishistic relationship to the telepistemological, asking again and again whether the people on our computer screens are "for real" or "faking it," and instead execute actions at a distance designed to alleviate the pain of others, whether that pain is "real" or not.

In this chapter, I have urged feminists to practice tele-ethicality as a way to derail the process by which women become virtualized. In Chapter Four, I explain the process of virtualization in greater detail, detailing how women such as camgirls are portrayed through the mass media as pornographic cyborgs, charged with violating boundaries between private and public in contemporary society.

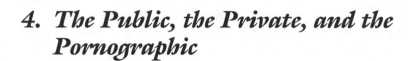

4. *The Public, the Private, and the Pornographic*

Are you always a good girl?
Show me your tits!
May I watch you?
Can U pet the CAT now??

I used to keep a list of the various ways people asked me to take my clothes off online, and the questions didn't end when I turned off the computer. The most disorienting approaches came from fellow academics, usually after we'd had a glass or two of wine at some function. "So," they would say as their eyes furtively swept the room, "do you ever, you know …?"

"Porn is inevitable with any new communication technology, from cave painting to the Internet," shrugs webcam viewer Alan. I'll note, however, that my friends who conduct research on internet file sharing don't have to field salacious questions every time they mention their work. Here, historian Walter Kendrick's point is made that more than a thing, pornography "names an argument" about social and economic power in a culture.[1] It is small wonder, then, that the camgirl—who traffics in a certain kind of power by violating the space between private and public—will always equated with pornography at some point in her life. The story that follows—about a radio show on which I was scheduled to appear as a camgirl 'expert'—makes this plain.

Cue the French Horns

My interview on National Public Radio began with the French horns that seem to begin all NPR broadcasts, followed by the scratchy voice-over of host Diane Rehm.[2] "Webcams were once the territory of the most cutting edge Internet users," Rehm told her listeners:

> Now, they are making their way into mainstream—for better and for worse. Joining us in Washington, Jeffrey Rosen from the George Washington Law

School. Rosen is the author of *The Unwanted Gaze*.[3] Joining us from New York, Terri Senft, instructor and Ph.D. candidate in Performance Studies, New York University. Joining us by phone, Amit Goswami, President, CEO and co-founder of SpotLife, an online personal broadcasting network.[4]

"Terri Senft," Diane Rehm croaked in my headset, summoning me to NPR's court of public opinion, "What many of us know about webcams is limited to more famous sites like JenniCam for exhibitionism and voyeurism. What has Jennifer Ringley done by putting herself on the Web the way she has?"

What had she done? "Well, Diane," I answered, "I am trying to examine webcamming as a form of women's expression. As far as Jennifer Ringley is concerned, I think she's inspired a number of people to put their own stories online. And of course, she's launched a huge controversy regarding how much to expose yourself in a technological environment."

"Jeffrey Rosen," Rehm pressed on. "We now have thousands of webcams. How are they being used, and who is watching?"

"People enjoy watching others in unguarded moments because it portrays a sense of power," replied Rosen, "and we can actually look down on others to some degree. ... Webcams are really part of this broader phenomenon exemplified by *Jerry Springer* and *Cops* in which ordinary people are taking the opportunity to turn themselves into celebrities."

"They are looking for that fifteen minutes of fame, Amit?" asked Rehm.

"We are giving power to consumers," Goswami countered, pointing out that although webcams can be used as surveillance mechanisms, SpotLife was about adding "high touch to high tech," helping bring together people in our increasingly isolated society.

Rosen responded that although Goswami's idea of high touch was alluring, it just "doesn't get to what's going on" with webcamming, because media environments are a "pseudo-environment in which the pictures in our head substitute for the reality of experience, so we aren't reaching out and touching those we know; we are being observed by strangers."

"And Terri," Rehm segued. "That's where you come in."

It was? I tried to figure out how to respond to a conversation that had jumped from the JenniCam to Jerry Springer to "observations by strangers" in five minutes. I began by explaining that we needed to separate volitional webcamming from more pernicious forms of online surveillance, such as Echelon (the international espionage satellite system)[5] and Carnivore (the FBI's Internet wiretapping system),[6] each of which predated the webcam by decades. I then mentioned that I had a webcam in my home myself.

Anticipating the questions that would come next, I told Rehm that my camera was basically a G-rated affair, and that I had long ago figured out how to avoid the cameras to dress. I talked about how webcammers have far more control over the production and dissemination of their image than appears at first glance, and how my site enabled me to connect to people with whom I would have never spoken otherwise.

"But why?" Rehm asked, as if I hadn't just answered that question. "Why do you allow yourself to be seen in this way? What are you after beyond communication? Is it your fifteen minutes of fame?"

It struck me that National Public Radio was as good a place as any to attempt to redirect the politics of this "But why?" question, so I asked Diane Rehm, "Why make a radio talk show?"

"Well, let's think about the differences," Jeff Rosen jumped in. "First of all, we are having a public discussion about a matter of public concern in a public place, as opposed to exposing our most intimate unguarded backstage behavior. The radio maintains that space between the public and private sphere, where the webcam breaches it. We are able to have a discourse undistracted by the voyeuristic appeal of prurience. We are not violating our own boundaries of privacy."

Whose Public?

There are a number of problems with Rosen's statement above, but I want to focus here on one: his use of the word 'public.' What exactly does it mean to declare oneself to be engaged in a public discussion about a matter of public concern in a public place, especially given that on National Public Radio, speakers, topics, and guests are chosen in advance and carefully scripted?

Queer theorist Michael Warner has argued that the term 'public' operates in three ways. The first is as *the* public, referring to everyone in the world.[7] The second is as *a* public, as in a crowd, or a theatrical audience. The third sense he describes as "the kind of public that comes into being only in relation to texts and their circulation—like the public of this essay."[8] Indeed, argues Warner, it is only through the circulation of texts (be they written, visual, or aural) that *a* public morphs into *the* public.[9]

The belief in publics from texts has its roots in eighteenth-century coffee houses in Europe, where the newly formed bourgeoisie gathered to discuss issues of the day. What made the original public sphere unique, stressed social theorist Jürgen Habermas, was its function as a "third space," separate from both home and business and their rigid hierarchies.[10] Freedom from hierarchy is what ultimately winds up fostering democracy—you may be my father at home, or my boss at work, but down at the pub, we are all equal, engaged in "communicative rationality."

The original public sphere was created by the media of its time—the penny newspapers and novels that were read, shared and debated in the coffeehouses. It was also bound by the social norms of its time: there were more than 3,000 coffee shops in London by the end of the eighteenth century, and women were forbidden from entering almost all of them. Today people are more apt to share links on the Web than they are newspapers, and (in America at least) men and women are online in near-equal numbers. Is it any wonder that a Google Scholar search for 'public sphere and internet' yields more 25,000 hits?

As exciting as the notion of a mediated public sphere is for some, our enthusiasm needs to be tempered.[11] If media were providing new public spheres, we would have an easier time conceptualizing ourselves as citizens with rights. Instead, increased media has led to a state Jodi Dean calls "communicative capitalism," with our chief rights being the 'right' to know and be known, the right to own and be owned, and the right to obsess over a truth 'out there' at the expense of reality 'in here.'[12]

In such a time, camgirls raise the question of whose public sphere we are talking about, anyway. They also remind us that the desire to exclude women from public life and designate their communication as strictly private is nothing new. Carolyn Dean, who reminds us that French revolutionaries routinely featured Marie Antoinette in pornographic pamphlets, explains that one of the most popular ways to lock a woman out of public discourse is to sexualize her body.[13] Lauren Berlant points out how pornography works as a discursive tool for conservatives, being "flashed in people's faces" as a way to freeze political activism around such issues as abortion, sexual harassment, sex workers' rights, and same-sex marriage, which are made to appear "ridiculous and even dangerous to the nation."[14] She calls this the creation of the intimate public sphere.

French horn music was firing up in the background again, which meant the Diane Rehm show was about to end. We were thanked for our participation and then cut off for the remainder of the broadcast. When I got home, my computer's screen showed an instant message from one of my friends. "Did you expect anything better from talk radio?" she asked. After a day or two, I realized my problem was that I *did* expect something better.

Whose Private? The Myth of the Free Exhibitionist

Turning away from the logic of Rosen and towards the work of Berlant, I would like to illustrate how the intimate 'public sphere' functions on the Web through what I call "the myth of the free online exhibitionist."

Camgirls are associated with exhibitionism as frequently as they are with voyeurism. When homecamming was in its heyday, I used to receive requests from reporters looking to interview women on the Web who pose live and nude, free of charge, simply because they "love sex." If the Web is not populated with attractive, good-hearted women willing to do sex work for free, reporters ask, how should we explain the fact that 78 percent of the adult material on the Web is located on free sites?[15]

In Chapter Two, I explained that sites featuring simulated voyeurism far outnumber sites featuring actual instances of voyeurism on the Web. The same holds true for exhibitionism. According to Rick Muenyong of the YNOT Adult Network, the majority of free exhibition sites on the Web are part of an elaborate network of click-through routes that ultimately lead to for-pay venues.[16] First, large companies seed the Web with sites designed to turn up at the top of the rankings when a surfer types 'young busty girls' or the like into a search engine such as Google. These sites give the viewer the impression that thousands of nude women are waiting out there for his or her viewing pleasure. This impression is magnified by the fact that images often link to one another in circular fashion as part of elaborate click-through arrangements between companies.

From the consumer's perspective, links remain free and plentiful, provided one is interested only in still images and the occasional twenty-second video snippet. What companies are hoping is that sooner or later, the customer will decide to pull out his credit card and pay to view the live women prominently advertised on the sites' retail front-end. The women they'll find at the end of a credit card transaction tend to fall into one of three categories: company girls, independents, and porn house girls.

Company Girls, Independents, and Porn House Girls

In Chapter Two, I explained that visitors hoping to get a live glimpse of a well-known Web porn personality such as Danni Ashe are usually disappointed. Instead, sites such as Danni's link to sites sponsored by companies who employ live women to interact with viewers. I call these women 'company girls.' "[The company I worked for] had three different sites," company girl Hanna (not her real name) told me.[17] "At the free site, women would sit around looking hot, sometimes flashing, and leaving [sex] toys in the frame suggestively." Hanna explained that all the seduction, flashing, and toys on the free site were designed to encourage men to purchase "private shows"—one-on-one sessions, charged by the minute, paid for with the customer's credit card. Hanna's employers paid her US$1 per minute for time spent in private shows, and nothing for time spent in free rooms convincing customers to buy shows. The amount of money she could make in a day varied. "I've made from US$60 in two hours to US$30 in four," Hanna recalled. Viewers were charged US$5–6 per minute for the shows.

A growing number of women are rejecting the company girl model of mediated sex work and instead choose to operate as independent agents through sites such as Internet Friends Network (iFriends).[18] iFriends dubs itself "the world's largest online video chat community" and its front page lists such chat topics as "gardening" and "online tutoring." Far and away its

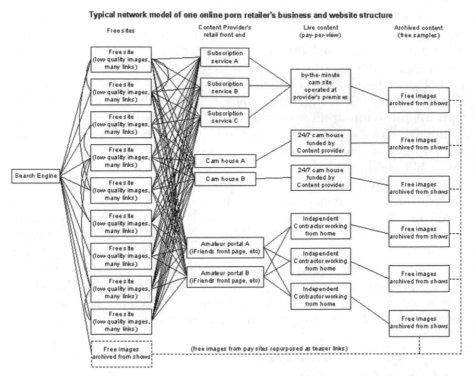

Figure 10. Typical network of an online porn retailer's business and Web structure. Note how the archived content (far right) gets recirculated into material for the free sites that turn up in a search engine (far left). Chart prepared by author.

largest user base, however, can be found in its Adults Only section, which groups women by age, build, bust size, ethnicity, hair color, eye color, height, and "special characteristics," including tattoos, piercings, and shaving.

Advertised with the slogan "The girl next door really *is* next door," iFriends allows women easy entry into the sex industry by handling their online credit card transactions and mailing out checks in discreet envelopes once a week. In contrast to live nude sites where workers are associated with company names, places such as iFriends encourage women to set their own prices for private shows, develop their own personal following, and build themselves as recognizable brands. "Get your clients to use your name often," women are told, "so they don't forget it and will return for future business."[19]

A third group of women—house girls—choose to live for months and even years at a time in houses equipped throughout with webcams. The best-known cam-house is Voyeur Dorm, which in 2003 opened with the message "Spy on us in our bedrooms, sneak a peek at us in our bathrooms, or just get to know us in our chat rooms."[20] "Get to know us in our chat rooms" is no throwaway line: contract players are expected to lure viewers into paying monthly subscriptions, which means they must build long-term relationships. At this writing, women of Voyeur Dorm (there are no men) get US$400–600 per week for their labors plus reimbursement for guitar lessons, karate classes, personal trainers, and the like—provided they take their lessons in the house.[21] In 2001 Voyeur Dorm claimed approximately 80,000 members paying US$34.95 per month each, with 40 percent paying an extra US$16 per month for "bonuses."[22]

In the early part of webcamming history, not all cam-houses were run as pornography businesses. As late as 2001, one could go to a site such as TheRealHouse (TRH) and hear viewers swearing that, for them, the attraction ranged from "not at all about porn" to "sex as a part of life" to "porn as a form of artistic expression."[23] As TRH founder John Styn explains, "I was intrigued by the possibilities of a cam-house infused with the interactivity of the CitizenX community. So I moved in new people and introduced the 'lifestyle as art' idea to the house."[24] Unfortunately, Styn's vision ultimately failed to pay the bills, and unlike the still-successful Voyeur Dorm, TRH closed its doors in 2002. "I shouldn't complain," Styn concedes. "Very few people are able to make a living by following dreams, because dreams usually have to be funded by work—'work' being anything you have to do when you'd rather be doing something else."

When You'd Rather be Doing Something Else

John's distinction between work and "something else" drives home what really keeps the fantasy of free exhibitionism alive on the Web: labor. In Chapter Two, I discussed Gavin Poynter's two categories of emotional laborers: professionals (such as therapists, salespeople, and teachers), who perceive themselves to be both capable of controlling their work environment and of equal standng with their customers, and nonprofessionals (such as checkout operators and call center employees), who do not.[25] I argued that although Poynter's distinction is useful to a point, it fails to account for the fact that in a networked world, the space between professional and nonprofessional laborers is rapidly collapsing.

Internet sex workers illustrate this observation nicely. On the one hand, they are drawn to this work because of its promise of safety and flexible hours. Hanna says that her employers "definitely presented themselves as being a protective kind of force, like they were the 'good guys' of the sex industry." As there was no regular busy time, she recalls, she was able to establish her own schedule in six-hour blocks, at her convenience. Yet even though Hanna was allowed to playfully reprimand abrasive people in chat rooms, any perception of worker equality with the customer ended once the private shows began. "Nothing about comfort level or personal desire was mentioned at all," she remembers. "You had to do whatever the customer said to get their money."

Hanna confessed to being especially disturbed by the fact that the moment a customer left her private room, she was immediately broadcast back into the public space. "So if you were naked and playing with some dildo everyone would see that for at least a few seconds." Repudiating the fantasy of the exhibitionist that led her customers to the site in the first place, Hanna explains, "I felt like I was fine doing that for money, but I wouldn't do it for free. Unless I am getting paid for it I have no incentive at all to do those things."

The fantasy of women gone wild on the Internet is fueled by the labor of real women in the online sex industry, but far from being news, the fact that everyone in network society exists in an *x* degrees of separation relationship to sex work is one of our biggest public secrets. Even American teenagers know as much: in a 2001 Kaiser Foundation survey, 70 percent of fifteen- to seventeen-year-olds admitted to accidentally coming across pornography on the Web, and a "sizable minority" (41 percent) described the experience as "no big deal."[26] Although it is perhaps comforting to know that American teens are not as traumatized by online pornography as the Religious Right might have us believe, is the omnipresence of highly visible, but never politicized, female sex workers truly "no big deal"? Is the intimate public sphere—with its creation, vilification, and "protection" of women like camgirls—the only possible way for us to live and work in network society?

Camp Performance and Counterpublic Critique

Political theorist Nancy Fraser has argued that throughout history, women have responded to their exclusion from the public sphere by establishing counter-publics, places where democracy is regularly critiqued and strengthened, not weakened as critics of women in public life often fear.[27] Fraser lists women's trade unions, alternative publishing forums, and feminist organizations as examples of counter-publics that consider the specificities of women's work and politics. Michael Warner argues that from a queer perspective, counter-publics are less "subalterns with reform programs" than groups who resist dominant culture through their performance, giving voice to what cannot be said in the public sphere.[28] Although it is difficult to see camgirls as counter-public in Fraser's sense, it may be possible to think of them this way in Warner's sense, particularly if we consider how they resist the intimate public sphere through their performance of strange familiarity.

In the 1970's, sociologist Stanley Milgram coined the term "familiar strangers" to refer to the relationship between people who know each other by sight but not by name in the public sphere, such as people from the same neighborhood who ride the train together at the same time each morning.[29] Even in our age of public cell-phone conversations, familiar strangers have kept up their tacit agreement not to engage with one another beyond a quick nod and a smile, as Intel researchers Eric Paulos and Elizabeth Goodman note.[30]

But does the same commitment not to engage exist when we find ourselves sitting on the train next to a woman whose webcam we were watching for five hours the night before? Does it apply when, after reading the blog of a boy who talks about being abused by his father, we suddenly and without warning find ourselves in a public space with the two of them? These scenarios move us from being familiar strangers to individuals bound in strange familiarity: the familiarity that arises from exchanging private information with people from whom we are otherwise remote.

As anyone who has ever sat on a crowded train can attest, negotiation with familiar strangers tends to be a largely dispassionate business. In contrast, strange familiarity tends toward the uncanny, the unnerving, and even the intimate. Camgirls reside in the realm of strange familiarity, and many of them manage such responses by turning to camp performance, which (when it works) has the power to morph the uncanny into a goofy in-joke everyone can enjoy.

Camp performance is a form of gender satire: it involves exaggerated portrayals of the features of men or women, it is designed to amuse, and it is often inappropriate—or at least naughty—in its presentations of 'reality.' In *Guilty Pleasures: Feminist Camp from Mae West to Madonna*, Pamela Robertson describes the feminist camp afficiando as one who "laughs at and plays with her own image by making fun of, and out of, that image—without losing real sight of the power that image has over her."[31]

For a few camgirls, camp is an overtly feminist tactic. Camgirls Ana Voog and Ducky Doolittle are both fans of feminist performance artist Annie Sprinkle, who has notoriously invited audience members to view her cervix using a speculum and a flashlight. By camping the masculine authority of the doctor's office, and allowing women and men to peer inside her body as if it were their own, Sprinkle made literal (and sexy) the title of *Speculum of the Other Woman*, a germinal feminist text.[32]

When I asked camgirl Melissa Gira (known online as Shakti), another Sprinkle fan, how she felt about the associations between camgirls and pornographers, she campily declared, "I want to be known as a pornographer. ... I crave it!"[33] For Gira, a Boston classics student and self-described "sacred whore," the Web enables her to stay "under the radar," in that "it allows me to have my anarchist, sex-radical agenda and still pay the bills." Indeed that is, she maintains, "the glory of the Net—it's so vast, one can hide revolutionary smut that hails women as the Goddess and it still reaches people, and they still pay for it."

Although Gira's argument for camgirl porn as camp "under the radar" feminism is undeniably alluring, it has limitations. To better understand why camgirl porn often fails as camp critique online, we should recall Chapter Two's discussion of camgirls as what Douglas Holt calls "cultural brands," designed to reconcile incompatible desires about sexual identity and economic change in a given era.[34] On the one hand, argues Holt, branding permits identifications that satisfy (or at least deflect) consumers' demands for greater participation in the economic and social policies structuring their lives. On the other, brands must serve the market before the consumer, which is why consuming 'ironically' or 'creatively' never works as political strategy.

"A Tale of Two Tampons": Part the First

Holt's argument is nicely transferred to what I call 'a tale of two tampons,' involving camgirls Lisa Batey and Ana Voog. Lisa, who worked at the camhouse HereandNow for nearly three years, consistently refused to be nude on camera, and even held her 'bathtub shows' in a bikini. For a time, Lisa's policy worked well, both for HereandNow's owner Erik Vidal and for their business partner Microsoft, which had a long-standing (if implicit) 'no porn' agreement with the cam-house. All this changed, however, the night Lisa focused her webcam on a used tampon in the toilet being flushed away with some paper. "I wasn't trying to be artsy or creative," she insists. "It wasn't even during a 'heavy time,' and I am sure from a distance you probably couldn't even tell if the thing was used or not. I just thought it was funny that there was a camera in the bathroom, and pointed it toward the toilet."[35]

Throughout this book, I have argued that the Web's aesthetic works less as a cinematic gaze or televisual glance than it does as a grab, noting that once an image travels to networked space, its reception and recirculation are entirely unpredictable. Lisa found this out the hard way when she gained the attention of the owner of the Stile Project, "a sort of porn-based 'gross out' site that had a lot of viewers," she recalls.[36] On the day she webcammed her tampon in the toilet, Stile pointed his viewers to HereandNow with the message "some girl ripped a bloody tampon out of her cunt and threw it in the toilet." As Lisa remembers it, immediately after Stile made the link, "there was this flood of people I've never seen in my chat room before yelling 'Shut up! Take your shirt off! Why are you even talking? You're so stupid,' etc. Just completely going off on me."

In truth, the sudden influx of Stile viewers wasn't a fluke but a planned event. To lure more advertisers to the site (and generate more revenue), HereandNow owner Erik Vidal had been courting the owner of Stile. Once Lisa realized the arrival of her new viewers was by design rather than by accident, she called for Vidal to intervene. As she recalls, Vidal "kept responding the same way, telling me that in order to get advertisers, they needed to show traffic figures, and our site looked better with the heavy traffic being brought in from Stile."

Once they realized Lisa had no intention of delivering the pornographic content they had been promised, Stile viewers drifted off. "To be fair," Lisa points out, "there were a couple people who wrote me later to say that although they first found out about our site from Stile, they stuck around because they thought what we were doing was cool." But overall, the move "caused bad feelings on all sides," Lisa remembers.

Part the second

In March 2001, self-described pro-porn camgirl Ana Voog was busy trying to put to rest a rumor that she was scamming fans for money to buy a house. Much of the hostility voiced by viewers had to do with a popular belief that camgirls get rich from doing nothing all day. In previous chapters, I explained the reasons for, and problems with, dismissing camgirl labor as doing nothing. Voog, who sees herself as fostering community on her site, listened to all opinions about how to raise money to buy a house until someone joked on a Usenet site, "Hell, for $1000 bucks, Ana better be prepared to bend over—and I don't mean to pick up my check!"[37]

On April 7, 2001, Voog posted three images to her LiveJournal. The first featured a vulva with a bloody tampon hanging from it and was captioned, "This is pussy." The second image featured a used tampon, full of fresh red blood, with a caption reading, "Gotta get me somma dat." The third was a shot of a pile of clipped pubic hair captioned, "Lonely? Need a pet? Try my pubic hair! On sale now! To the highest bidder!!!"[38] For those sympathetic to Voog, it was easy to see her triptych as a counterpublic response to the call to "bend over." Ana's first image is reminiscent of "The Red Flag," a 1971 piece by feminist artist Judy Chicago that featured a used tampon.[39] Yet whereas Chicago's work was intended as a way to celebrate the natural female body, Ana's captions evoked the hard-core style of feminist performance artist Karen Finley. The inherent humor of the piece is vintage Annie Sprinkle. "[I was] uncomfortable for a few seconds," admits viewer Frank (known online as Grass). "Then my mind said: Why not? Get their attention first, and then make the sales pitch. How much for the trimmings?"[40]

Yet Ana's triptych didn't just grab its audience; it was also grabbed by them, rippling through the networks in which Ana worked, played, and lived in ways she could not have anticipated. The day after she posted it, Ana received an email from the LiveJournal Abuse Team (charged with maintaining LiveJournal's terms of service) describing her images as "quite frankly, vulgar." The team requested that Ana take her images off Live-Journal. "Note that artistic nudity is given broad consideration," the email advised, "but this is by no means artistic in any way."[41]

The moment Ana received the email, she wrote a lengthy reply in which she urged viewers to protest attempts to censor her online. She dramatically titled her post *"WOMEN'S BODIES/CYCLES SILENCED AGAIN!!!!!!!!!!!!!!!!!!! NO MORE!!!!!!!!!!!!!"* Approximately eighty posts later, the LiveJournal Abuse Team relented, and Ana's photos were allowed to stand.[42] Anti-censorship campaigns on the Web are a sure way to garner attention, and once LiveJournal moved to censor Ana Voog, hers was an easy argument to win. In a way, this was a shame. When any exchange gets sidetracked with legalisms, it's almost impossible to return to the conversations at hand, however interesting they may have been.

And the conversation about the appearance of Ana's words and images on people's Friends Pages was very interesting indeed. Earlier in this chapter, I explained how reading morphs *a* public into *the* public through the circulation of texts, as in the phrase "public opinion." In a similar way, most people derive their understanding of what LiveJournal is exclusively from reading their personalized Friends Page. Among LiveJournal readers, a general feeling seems to prevail that although one's personal Web site is theater watched by silent viewers who come and go at will, and one's personal LiveJournal page is similar to a living room into which one invites people in the neighborhood for cocktails, one's Friends Page is better thought of as the assembly of neighbors themselves.[43]

Once this is understood, it is relatively easy to understand why LiveJournal users supported Ana's right to express herself on her LiveJournal, yet displayed a "not in my backyard" attitude when her photos showed up on their LiveJournal Friends Page. For the sizable percentage of LiveJournal users who read their Friends Page at work, Ana's triptych was the equivalent not of going to see a sexually edgy camp performer such as Annie Sprinkle but of having Annie Sprinkle turn up at your office unannounced to stage an impromptu show in front of your colleagues.

Pushing the Limits: Young Girls on the Web

Up to this point, I have been issuing a twofold warning regarding the limits of feminist porn-as-camp on the Web. First, feminist porn—even porn meant to be camp—must contend with the dialectics of the market. Second, camp subjected to the aesthetics of the grab loses much of its force as it circulates through networks where it is hard to tell where 'our' counterpublic space ends and 'my' privatized personal Friends Page begins.

I now turn my attention to what I see as a limit case for those who advocate porn as counterpublic camp on the Web: the rise of underage camgirls who encourage their (mostly older, almost entirely male) fans to buy them gifts on sites such as Amazon in exchange for on-camera flirtations. In her piece on the topic for *Salon*, Katharine Mieszkowski described "cam whores" (a name they use for themselves) as "kids who understand what power they have ... to titillate and suggest, with just a smile, or a bit of a tummy, or more."[44]

Why is it so hard for me to see cam whoring as counterpublic expression? Even as I make the argument, I hear the voice in my head, saying. "Yes, that's fine for us. But what happens when we talk about the predators? As feminists interested in protecting the children, we cannot be blind to the fact of *them.*"

I want to argue that this is a dangerous line of communication, whether practiced by journalists or academics. First, it assumes that there is a 'we' who would never find a child desirable, even though we live in a culture predicated on youth worship, and even though desiring and acting are not the same thing. As James Kinkaid explains:

> We see children as, among other things, sweet, innocent, vacant, smooth-skinned, spontaneous, and mischievous. We construct the desirable as, among other things, sweet, innocent, vacant, smooth-skinned, spontaneous, and mischievous. There's more to how we construct the child, and more to how we construct what is sexually desirable—but not much more.[45]

In terms reminiscent of Berlant's "intimate public" Kinkaid makes a similar observation regarding what he terms the "Gothic horror narrative" of child sexual abuse, noting that "we have become so engaged with tales of childhood eroticism (molestation, incest, abduction, pornography) that we have come to take for granted the irrepressible allure of children. We allow so much power to the child's sexual appeal that we no longer question whether adults are drawn to children ..."[46]

Even more disturbing is the way this line of logic forecloses is the way it forecloses any discussion of how feminism might serve sexually active teens and pre-teens. Steven Angelides argues that the rigid characterization of all child-child sexuality as "exploration" and all adult-child sexuality as "exploitation" fails to accurately characterize a wide range of alternative sexual histories, such as those experienced by members of the gay male community.[47] At its most ludicrous, cultural blindness to the fact that children can and do engage in adult-like sexual expression leads to incidents like the 2006 case in which two New England teen girls were charged with child pornography for circulating nude photos of *themselves* on Myspace.[48]

In his plea for a more realistic understanding of children, Angelides recommends that we stop conceptualizing child sexuality in terms of danger and/or play. Instead, he suggests the categories of risk and—yes—pleasure. I likewise believe that when talk about phenomena like cam whoring, we might do well to tone down our focus on identity play and pedophile danger, and instead talk about the risks and, again, pleasures of many-to-many communication. This will involve some committed reframing of the issues.

As in the 'tale of two tampons,' the problem with conceptualizing cam whores as counterpublic communities has less to do with the individuals in question than it does with the networks in which they circulate. In Chapter Two, I argued that rather than a new form of voyeurism, Web grabbing is better understood through the mechanics of "commodity fetishism," a term used by Karl Marx to describe what happens when consumers begin affording manufactured objects with something like subjectivity. Commodities obey the logic not of subjects, but of the market, which is why it makes little sense to ask what the cam whore phenomenon 'means' outside of the Web economy in which it exists.

There are three interrelated sets of myths and facts that fuel this economy online. The first myth is that there is a massive financial market for child pornography on the Web. The fact is, nobody sells child porn—at least not for long. In law enforcement circles, they joke that the only person who will offer to sell you child pornography is another law enforcement officer. This is not to say that there isn't child pornography on the Web, because there is—and a lot of it. It may horrify those writers who extol the virtues of the gift economy, but swapping data isn't just for Linux programmers: it's the primary means by which pedophiles obtain images on the Web.[49]

The second myth—the myth of the free exhibitionist, discussed earlier—is structurally the inverse of the first. Just as the 'child porn economy' turns out to run on uncompensated labor, so 'free exhibitionism' is fueled by for-pay sex work. The third myth—the 'white child seduced into sex slavery' myth—likewise depends for its existence on the denial of some very plain truths.

It is true that children have been befriended by adults on the Web who have lured them into sexual activities both online and off. Unquestionably, this sort of behavior is reprehensible, and such adults should absolutely be punished to the fullest extent of the law. But the reason mainstream media report so much on these cases is precisely because they are isolated. The truth is that on almost all American 'Lolita porn' sites which send spam, the models look young, but must sign documents attesting to the fact that they are at least twenty-one years old.

By contrast, on the private section of escort review sites like BigDoggie.com, one gets the distinct impression that the 'women' mentioned in members' Amazon-style reviews of sex tourist trips actually *are* young.[50] This is because the real story—the one that hides in plain sight—is that the Web is being used to to arrange for child sex work in places like Thailand, Cuba, Ghana and elsewhere.

In pointing out the realities of how the Web may assist those engaged in sex tourism and trafficking, I don't want to replicate the same moral panics I've been objecting to throughout this chapter. As Jo Dozema points out, even among feminists, there exists a determination to divide sex workers into two categories: 'adults' who 'choose' to work, and 'children' who are 'forced'.[51] Not only do distinctions of this type beg the question of choice and force, Dozema argues, but they also reinforce the Madonna/whore distinction the women's liberation movement was supposed to eradicate.

Heather Montgomery, whose research involves child sex workers in Thailand, agrees, explaining how public interest in child sex "frequently has the effect of harnessing prurient horror for political ends, which often substitute understanding for sensationalism and moral outrage."[52] In terms reminiscent of Laurent Berlant's intimate public sphere, Montgomery points out that sensationalist accounts of child sex work have created a climate in which the observations and testimony of "individual children who sell sex have been largely overlooked."[53]

At this point, you may be thinking that this conversation has moved a long way from cam whores on the Web. In terms of linear narrative, you are of course correct. But if we think in terms of networks, the connections become clear: the 'innocent' child, exposed to the same porn spam as the rest of us, who decides to make the most of her flirting skills to acquire gifts off Amazon; the twenty-one-year-old professional actress who self-presents as a fifteen-year-old amateur video maker on YouTube; the Web surfer who knows very well he won't get something for nothing on the Web, but keeps clicking just the same; the internationally notorious Canadian pedophile who a friend of mine realized she had befriended on FaceBook; the voices of consumers on sex tourism sites and the voices of 'school girl' sex workers in Japan as they finally tell their stories to one another through their own social networking sites—we are all, as the broadband companies keep telling us, connected.

Toward a Politics of Relationality

By this point, it should be clear that I think current attitudes toward teen sexual expression and the Web need some serious re-thinking. Still, it feels wrong to take an entirely laissez-faire attitude. How, then, should we respond? Postcolonial critic Ella Shohat warns that "I'm OK, you're OK" cultural relativism freezes dialogue among disagreeing parties just as effectively as universalism does.[54] Instead, she urges feminists to begin looking at our lives relationally. Shohat explains that her argument is not that we are all different, but that histories and communities exist in "co-implicated" networks, the nodes of which offer "mutual illumination" when juxtaposed for analysis.

I think of Shohat's words when I hear testimony from older camgirls talking about younger ones. "People said I would be ashamed of myself, that those images would haunt me," explains Ducky, who began appearing in adult magazines thirteen years ago.[55] "I thought they were crazy, that the magazines would be off the racks in a month and eventually disappear altogether." As it happens, she admits, people still recognize her from topless motorcycle magazines she posed for in the late 1980's. "Luckily I am totally shameless!" she says, "but other people change, and I worry that some of these women don't recognize the long-term effects of broadcasting your image."

"If I'd been doing webcamming a couple of years ago, I think it would have had some very negative effects on my self-image and self-esteem," confessed Lux, who was at the time a twenty-one-old camgirl and sex work activist.[56] Lux points out, "When you learn about the power of sex appeal at a young age, sex appeal starts to look like it's your *only* power," and worries, "What if a camgirl takes it personally, and feels that people aren't interested in her because there's something wrong with her? I just think that the younger you are, the more at risk you are for … damage."

Even when it is difficult, I try to respect the ways in which people make sense of their own lives, based on the information they have available to them, bound by the times in which they find themselves living. Though I am not one myself, I also try to remember that parents count as people, too. For those who have perhaps found the last few pages upsetting, I wanted to offer a story that demonstrates how at least one Web viewer made a choice to engage with me in a way that exemplifies Shohat's notion of a relational, rather than a universal, approach to identity and community.

Ira's Story

Nearly a year and a half after my first exposure to camgirl Ana Voog's Web site, she and I became friendly enough that we decided to meet in New York at the home of camgirl Stacy Pershall, the star of Atomcam. Needless to say, the whole affair was webcast as it happened (but not streamed, so there were no sounds to be heard, only images to be seen). That night, as

I drank beer and did girly things, a man I had not previously met watched me online. He emailed me the URL to his LiveJournal the next day, saying that my online presence the previous night had "impacted" him. Curious, I went to read what he wrote. I found it so powerful I want to print it here, with his permission:

> It's 3 am and I am on the computer. What's worse is that the whole time I've been sitting here piddling about on Photoshop, I've had Stacy's (atomcam.com) window open and I've been watching her and Ana (AnaCam.com) and some short-haired brunette go about the things that 20something girls do together in NYC apartments in November.
>
> It's not a sex thing, first off. Everyone had their pants on, including me. I've long since stopped masturbating at the Internet. But it is a cam girl, and it is a human connection for these hours when I feel like the light from me would take a million years to get to anyone. The [computer] window has 4 screens, two in the living/bedroom, one kitchen, and one at the PC. The girls are everywhere. The cats are everywhere. It's like a slumber party because Ana is visiting Stacy and it's all linked up and stuff.
>
> I find out that the mystery brunette is "Terri" and she's doing her doctorate on cam girls and she's hanging out with these two and having a great old time and drinking beer and all of that. When she goes back to the girls, I slip over to Terri's page. I am looking for short story stuff for FENCE (magazine I edit), and the front of her home page assures me that her writing isn't like that, that she writes "academic" something. I go anyway.
>
> While I have this girl in my window, I am scanning her works. Co-author here, book here, columnist here. Jesus. It's a bit intimidating. She's probably six years younger than me, and I call myself a writer. But in the midst of all of this academic sexuality, Internet discourse, & feminist topics I recognize, I find that one that thing that jumps out at me, especially at 2:30 am. "My experience with phone sex" (or something to that effect.) Naturally, I look.
>
> Soon, I am reading. I feel like I've hit the wrong link, that I've glitched my way into a private diary, but no, this is put online for me to read. I am reading of a young woman with a dying mother and a cardboard father. I am reading of lonely northern snow in an absent town and a girl who didn't have a good thing to say about anything, who was ready to die the day her mom did. It is too personal. My feet scuffle the floor of her mother's empty apartment. I can feel the drafts of Buffalo wind at the hospital windows. And the sex part? In part of the story she wrote, she talked of masturbating. She masturbated, she talked to women, she came and came. And I wasn't excited at all.
>
> As I was reading, and even as I type this, I am watching Terri laugh and roll around 1200 miles away. In my computer window, I have this normal-looking girl in cropped black top, black bra and khakis, barefoot and sleepy, mussed up hair and post-drunk laughing grin. On the page I have line after line of writing works and dialogue that makes my balls retract in shame that I've done so little in my time with all that I have. And in spite of the fact that she's very pretty, and very alluring in her cropped top and bare feet I don't think of her frantic fingers

as she juggles the phone. I should. A masturbating woman is usually a real turn on for me, but right now its not.

Even as I type this she's looking at the camera through a red gel that Ana has put over the lens. And I know she can't see me, and that her mother dying just before Christmas is the last thing on her mind right now. But it's on mine. I am watching her for real, but I felt like I have broken into her head. This doesn't make sense unless you read the story, and with her permission I'll post the link.

But after this surreal experience, all I think is "raw"
raw sex
and raw loss

I think of her emotion, the blind cast into the ether of her loss, of her urge, of how she copes. I came here expecting sex. Expecting something base, something to bring this girl to ground a bit. But not like this. I know why, but I don't understand why. And she has no idea any of this is happening.[57]

"It makes little sense to think of the World Wide Web as a global public space," maintain William Davies and James Crabtree, "because there is little evidence of a global public to occupy it."[58] Rather, they argue, the Web is a series of "quasi-public" neighborhoods "rife with familiar strangers."[59] In addition, as I have been arguing, it is full of strange familiarities: intimacies that cannot be avoided and must in some way be negotiated. "At the neighborhood level," Davies and Crabtree write, "it is shared problems that link 'space' to 'place,' that relate individuals to local communities."[60]

In a sense, Ira is someone who finds himself wandering past my storefront in his neighborhood and then heads through the door, to the back and into my stockroom to poke around. He sees my silent image on a screen and gets curious. He goes to my Web site and looks at my credentials, the pieces of paper I've had to amass to be invited on to National Public Radio. He is intimidated by the résumé but intrigued by the sex. He begins to read my essay, the story of the most painful experience of my life. It is about my mother's death from brain cancer just before Christmas. His mother, who just died the previous year, had her birthday Christmas day. I am not hiding my sexuality. He's not hiding his predilection for it. But there is something bigger going on.

Up to this point, Ira is responding to the drama in front of him in classic Aristotelian fashion, making connections to his own life in hopes of achieving catharsis. Then something else happens. He looks at the screen and understands with undeniable clarity that *I am clearly not him, and yet I am*—at least to some degree. He thinks about being "in my head," and the responsibility this imposes on him, the reader—the potential friend, even. He then chooses to chronicle his experience watching and reading me on his LiveJournal, linking to my LiveJournal, which further networks us for anyone interested in following the connections. He writes me personally, in case I don't realize he has connected to me. Later, I read his work, write back to him, and mark him as a LiveJournal friend.

Feminists seeking to meld the personal and the political in a time of networks need to proceed the way Ira does. Rather than being shocked by or naïvely endorsing the lives we see playing out in front of us in the storefront displays in our mediated neighborhoods, we need to take the time to stop and look around the premises. When we communicate what we are seeing to the people we are watching, we need to understand that ours can only ever be a partial understanding of the situation, screened through our own desires. Most important, we need to make it clear that our objective is connection—however halting and confused that connection might be—rather than a debate about 'problems.' Connections aren't made abstractly, but through individuals. In network society, opportunities abound for making contact at the individual level and, in so doing, affecting the world at large. In Chapter Five, I continue my exploration of trust in networked environments, both on and offline.

5. I Am a Network: From 'Friends' to Friends

In the winter of 1994, my mother accused me of giving her brain cancer, and asked me to leave the hospital room where she lay dying. Her request left me utterly isolated, bereft of the company of my mother, the other caretakers on the cancer ward, and—because I had taken a leave of absence from school months earlier—my fellow graduate students. I had occasional contact with my brothers, but they were busy trying to hold down jobs while covering the work that I had been doing for my mother before she turned me away. Although I managed to fill my days, the nights were unrelentingly lonely.

Too ashamed to join a cancer support group or find a therapist, I aimlessly tried to connect with people in a variety of ways: writing classes, bars, phone sex lines. One night I discovered that I could use my computer and a modem to reach other people. The first site I ever visited was an online sex bulletin board called Cyberoticom. Users of other 'adult' chat services in those early days of the internet will be unsurprised to learn that nearly all erotic conversation there was quickly subsumed by tech talk and banter.

Because I am good with words, some of the users on the site told me about Echo, an online bulletin board system where people gathered to discuss things like books, politics, film and New York City. One of them told me that the *Village Voice* had dubbed Echo 'The Algonquin Round Table of Cyberspace.' Even more appealing was the fact that Echo members met once a week at a local bar to socialize. Although anyone could join Echo, my Cyberoticom friends told me they would vouch for me, giving me access to the secret, 'elite' areas on the system.

There was one catch, though: I couldn't say where we'd met. Even though there seemed to be considerable overlap between the members of Echo and Cyberoticom, it was important to my new friends that their dual identities remain separate. So when I joined Echo, I honored their desire to remain in the closet as sex chat aficionados. But after Cyberoticom closed in 1996, they broke their own silence. Suddenly, our sordid beginnings seemed more funny than scandalous. We had established our community on Echo—how we had gotten there was no longer the point.

Such are the strange turns our networks take. Throughout this book, I have been speaking about tele-ethicality: a commitment to risk enagement, rather than forestall action, in our mediated communities, despite the potential for fakery and fraud. I begin this chapter with a story about myself rather than one about a camgirl because I want to be able to speak to those risks—and rewards—in the first person. Although first-hand dissolutions of our social networks can be devastating at the time they occur, tele-ethical practice can help reframe losses as growth experiences. The reframing can be immediate, or it can take years. Sometimes those directly involved with the initial incident will be long gone, and impossible to contact. Other times, our past haunts us in the form of new people with new issues.

One cannot avoid issues of trust in networked environments, particularly with regard to friendships. Although trust always involves risk, I warn against over-reliance on reputation system software to manage our online contacts. Instead, I turn to the original friend of camgirls—LiveJournal—and its concept of 'friending,' which explicitly requires users to consider issues of power and control in their negotiations with others. The first part of this chapter ends by considering LiveJournal's reputation among bloggers, focusing especially on LiveJournal's relegation to the ghetto of the personal. I then use stories from LiveJournal members to explore (and advocate) a form of activism I call 'networked reflective solidarity': a kind of political identification that hails the viewer/listener as "one of us" while insisting that one cannot ever know everything about anyone.

On Social Capital and Reputation

These days, it is difficult to have a academic conversation about a site like Facebook or LiveJournal without someone bringing up the issue of social capital. Simply put, the theory of social capital maintains that we draw value from our social contacts with other human beings. "Just as a screwdriver (physical capital) or a college education (human capital) can increase productivity (both individual and collective), so too social contacts affect the productivity of individuals and groups," writes Robert Putnam.[1]

Huysman and Wulf explain the wide permit of social capital when they write, "Social capital refers to network ties of goodwill, mutual support, shared language, shared norms, social trust, and a sense of mutual obligation that people can derive value from. It is understood as the glue that holds together social aggregates such as networks of personal relationships, communities, regions, or even whole nations."[2]

In *Bowling Alone,* Putnam argues that the kind of social capital that enabled things like parent-teacher associations or consciousness-raising groups is on the decline, at least in America.[3] Many who agree with Putnam are quick to blame technology, claiming that people are spending more time watching their televisions and computer screens than communicating with one another. As one might expect, a number of Internet researchers have taken the opposite position.

"Internet use is adding on to other forms of communication, rather than replacing them," argue Barry Wellman et al., contending that social capital is moving away from local communities bounded by geography and toward the Web in the form of "networked individualism." As communications devices become smaller and more mobile, Wellman et al. suggest, "Connections are to people and not to places," which means "the technology affords shifting of work and community ties from linking people-in-places to linking people at any place…The person has become the portal."[4]

That people are now portals to multiple communities creates new challenges, particularly in regard to gatekeeping: If vouching for others is no longer a function of the neighborhood or the association, on whom can we rely when it comes time to admit someone new? Enter reputation management systems designed to help us measure the value of others. Seller/buyer ratings on eBay,[5] the "karma" system on "Slashdot"[6] and Daily Kos diary recommendations[7] are examples of fairly effective reputation systems.

Certainly, when one is purchasing a product or looking for the answer to a technical question, reputation systems can be useful. But for those of us who have been attracted to the power of networks as a way to complicate traditional political models, the celebration of reputation systems is troubling. By necessity, these systems reinforce what Andy Blunden calls the "ultimate commodity fetishism": the belief that human relationships within networks can be quantified as if they were material goods.[8] By counting, tallying, and hoarding human interactions as currency, Blunden argues, proponents of social capital ultimately stall truly progressive social action in networked environments by fostering cliquishness and cronyism instead of open, serendipitous exchange.

Will You Be My Friend?
Social Networks, Friendship and Trust

On most social networking sites, there are no reputation systems. Instead, there is 'friending': the act of adding people to one's Friends network. The process of friending differs from space to space, but on LiveJournal, I choose friends by adding someone's name to a list. From that point forward, their public posts will show up on my Friends Page when I read each

ay. Other users may likewise befriend me. If I mutually agree to the friendship, they have access to 'friends only' portions of my LiveJournal. If not,
they are restricted to the same public entries that everyone else can read.

As danah boyd observes, the costs of befriending someone vary from
space to space in social networking circles. On sites like MySpace and
Friendster, she notes, "there is little to lose by being loose with Friendship
and more to gain."[9] Friendship is a somewhat more fraught business on
LiveJournal, in part because mutual friendship grants entry to our not-
for-the-general-public postings on the system. In their study of how people
befriend one another on LiveJournal, Kate Raynes-Goldie and David Fono
found friendship had a wide range of meanings ranging from content (people one likes to read), offline facilitators (people one knows in real life),
online communities, a show of trust, a courtesy, a declaration, or nothing
at all.[10] My own LiveJournal friends are a mix of people I know well in my
offline life, people working in my field, people I have never met with interesting LiveJournals, and former students. (I do not allow current students
on my Friends List.) No matter what their back-story, on LiveJournal, these
people are all simply my "friends."

Both online and offline, the decision to befriend someone is an act of
trust. But in our offline lives, we tend to make such decisions gradually, con-
ditionally, and implicitly. We don't, except in rare instances, meet someone
and immediately declare her our friend—it's not a determination we're
often called upon to make, and not one we necessarily give much thought
to in the early stages of a friendship. By contrast, on LiveJournal, the decision to, 'friend,' is frequently vexed, because it is both explicit and public.
How is it that we make the determination to trust someone online?

In any relationship, online or off, our decisions about whom to trust and
how much depend on both our conscious and our unconscious responses
to the self-representations of others. We are operating in the conscious
realm when we dismiss as spam the email claiming to be from our bank that
is riddled with grammatical errors. We are operating from the unconscious
when something unnamed about one person just doesn't sit right with us,
or when we get a 'good feeling' about another. Online and off, we are more
likely to trust, for instance, a 'friend of a friend,' for reasons both rational
and irrational—when we meet someone offline who has the imprimatur of
another friendship, we are likely to extend ourselves to that person without
much deliberation.

This impulsive, instinctive quality of trust is one reason why the act of
befriending people in online social networks causes angst and consterna-
tion. When someone asks me to acknowledge her as a member of one of my
online social networks, she is requesting explicit affirmation—a conscious,
overt decision of a kind that I usually leave to my social autopilot. If I grant
that acknowledgement, I am not just extending trust, I am *announcing* that

I am extending trust, and implicitly encouraging others in my network to do so as well.

On the other hand, if I refuse to acknowledge her as part of my network, or even delay responding to her request, I run the risk of upsetting or offending her—and, by extension, the friends with whom she is networked. Just as I will appear to be vouching for her if I befriend her, my friends are on some level vouching for her now, and I must decide whether to bring her into my circle or to exclude her from it.

As fraught as the decision to friend (or not) is, the decision to 'defriend' is more challenging still. In the offline world, friendships and acquaintance-ships rarely end with a declaration, but on a site like LiveJournal there is no other way *for* them to end, unless one party to the relationship leaves the network entirely. Defriending is such an issue on LiveJournal that some people post entire essays on their friending policies. Others periodically announce that they are going through a 'friends purge,' most frequently justified on the grounds their list has gotten too unwieldy. Whatever the stated reason for the defriending, some will inevitably take the act as a personal rejection.

These concerns may seem overly dramatic to those who have not spent much time in networked online space, or to those whose social networks are small. But even small circles become exceedingly complex as they begin to expand—as the number of individuals in a network grows arithmetically, the number of relationships in that web grows geometrically. And the larger the network, the blurrier it is at the edges. A comment that I leave on a friend's LiveJournal will not be read only by our mutual friends, but by the members of that person's other circles of trust. Even as we recognize our obligation to take responsibility for what we say in such settings, we may realize that we have little control over how it is heard, circulated, and acted upon. The decision to extend trust in such an environment is a momentous and intimidating one.

In her essay on the topic of friending, danah boyd warns of four long-term concerns with which social scientists must wrestle in their research on social networks.[11] First, there is the issue of persistence: of information we'd prefer be forgotten, and of persistence access by those we may later want denied from our networks. Next is the searchability of our networked connections: in a time of conspicuous connection, viewers tracing our 'chains of friendship' may come to conclusions about us we would prefer they not. There is also the issue of replicability: it is important to remember that the age of digital reproduction brought us 'Fakesters' as well as 'Friendsters.' Finally, there is the fact that for all our attempts to limit and address viewers as friends, a large portion of our words and images will go before unknown, unseen strangers.

Still, in spite of all its complexity and potential for drama, I prefer 'friending' to reputation systems. For me, a LiveJournal 'friend' is an excellent example of a catachresis—a word that is deliberately misused for rhetorical effect. We now provide video and audio to make our online friendships more closely develop offline ones. Why should we try to mitigate ambiguity when it is the most natural thing of all? Friendship on Facebook is considered so complex that pre-cooked options include check boxes marked "lived together," "through friend," "through Facebook," "met randomly," "we hooked up," "we dated," and—my favorite—"I don't even know this person." When I am out with a casual acquaintance, and we run into my closest companion of ten years, I introduce them to one another as friends, as in, "Angus, this is my friend, Kim." I may provide more context, but I may not, and I certainly don't produce a pop-up window with tick boxes that identify how I know these people.

Will You be My Community?
The Case of 'WeirdJews'

Just as we introduce varying people as simply 'friends,' so too do we speak of our 'community' in concrete and abstract ways. Nobody expects us to know everyone in our gay community, and as Benedict Anderson notes, there is a strategic reason for this: if I had to know each person in my imagined community before doing anything on behalf of others, political action would cease to exist.[12] To use computer jargon, vagueness in defining our friends and community shouldn't be viewed as a bug, but rather a feature.

In the spring of 2006, I was invited to speak at the annual meeting of the Association of Jewish Funders. Older members of the organization were concerned that younger Jews seemed more interested in the Internet than in going to synagogue, and they were hoping I could enlighten them as to why this might be the case. I agreed to do some asking around the online communities with which I was familiar, and to let them know what responses I got to their question.

Not sure of where to start, I posed the question to my LiveJournal readers. Soon, someone replied, "You know who would be great for this? The LiveJournal WeirdJews group."[13] I went to the WeirdJews community, which carries the tag line "Disrupting Yeshivas since 2002." The group had about a thousand members, and received roughly half a dozen posts a day. I read their introduction:

> A community for Jews outside the mainstream. All "Weird Jews" are welcome here whether they be Orthodox, Conservative, Reform, Reconstructionist, born-Jews, Jews by Choice, or anyone considering conversion...We usually let almost everyone join unless given a good reason not to. (ex: neo-Nazi's, proselytizing Christians, banned ex-members under different names). Once you've joined, go ahead and introduce yourself. Most of us have made friends from this community both on LJ and in real life. You'll be glad you did so.

I decided to ask the question, "Why did you turn to WeirdJews?" I was told
that one of the biggest challenges for young Jewish people moving away
from home is that not every small town in America has a synagogue they'll
feel comfortable in, and not every student has the time to try and fit into
a community in a town she'll be leaving in a few years. Young people were
also concerned about not feeling 'Jewish enough,' either because of tattoos,
piercings, queerness, non-observance of Jewish tradition, or what I came to
call 'the Mother question' (a person's birthright claim to Judaism is passed
through her mother). Another challenge was one of finances: joining a synagogue can be costly, and many students didn't feel they had the 'right' to
worship in a place where they couldn't pay dues.

     Still another—and for some people, critical—issue was the relationship
between Judaism and Zionism. Many of the group felt certain that their
anti-Zionist views would be unwelcome in synagogue, and expressed a desire
for political affinity with like-minded people. Others expressed a desire to
speak with those unlike themselves in a safe environment. Time and again,
people would say things like, "If I walked into an Orthodox shul and told
them what I thought about some of their traditions or even asked them
about them I'd be encouraged to leave and I would be the topic of conversation afterwards. But because I have a forum, I can talk about these things."

     When I asked the question, "Why use online forums?" I could not have
gotten a better answer than the one I received from WeirdJews community
member Ephraim Oakes. "The communication tools produce discussion,
they allow emphases or perspectives radically different from one's own, and
they're a starting point for do-it-your-own culture building that is not necessarily beholden to the political or religious or cultural agendas of mainstream institutions and their funding."[14]

     The do-it-yourself culture building Oakes mentions above is simply micro-
politics by another name. Watching members of WeirdJews interact with one
another, it was obvious to me that theirs was an explicitly Jewish community,
synagogue or not, just as a consciousness-raising group is a feminist community, with or without an explicit political agenda. A historical reading of
grass-roots politics shows that activism often springs not from institutions but
from groups of like-minded people in such 'non-political' spaces as college
dormitories, churches, and gay bars. These communities may not have been
designed for political action, but they have often facilitated it.

Personal Journals and Narcissism

Given the contested nature of terms like 'friend' and 'community' in social
networks like LiveJournal, it seems odd that more academic work hasn't
focused on them. In a discussion of personal 'journals' versus overtly political 'blogs,' Susan Herring asks how the most common blog type (personal

journals) "could be so overlooked and underrepresented in discussions about the nature of blogs."[15] Although Herring and her team don't offer any clear-cut explanations, they do note that personal blogging is a disproportionately female and youth-dominated pursuit.[16] This is certainly borne out on LiveJournal, where women outnumber men 2:1 and most users are between the ages of fifteen and twenty-one.[17]

Perhaps because of their demographics, personal journals seem more susceptible than political blogs to charges of narcissism among their users. Although the Narcissus of ancient Greek myth was male, in psychoanalytical theory narcissism was originally associated with the feminine. To Freud, women and gay men were particularly susceptible to infantile self-absorption and pre-occupation with their own image, and thus more likely to be pathologically narcissistic.[18] This feminization of narcissism persists today in popular conceptions of blogging. Personal blogs, a disproportionately feminine genre, are often seen as narcissistic, though self-absorption and vanity are not notably absent from the psychological makeup of the politics-obsessed.

In a 1993 essay, Gayatri Spivak explored the gendered uses to which Narcissus has been put, turning back to Ovid to ask, "What of the woman in Narcissus's story?"[19] She recalls Echo, the mountain nymph who falls in love with Narcisssus. Long ago, Echo had helped Zeus conduct romantic affairs by distracting his wife, Hera, with her chatter, and Hera had punished her by making Echo unable to speak, except to repeat the last words said to her. "You shall still have the last word, but no power to speak first," Hera told Echo.[20]

When Echo sees Narcissus, she is smitten. She wants to speak to him, but can only repeat his last word to her. When he rejects her, she pines for him until nothing is left of her but her voice. Spivak argues that "the account of Echo is the story of a punishment that is finally a dubious reward quite outside the borders of the self." As she puts it, "Narcissus is fixed, but Echo can disseminate."[21]

When I first read Spivak's words, I was confused, but later, when thinking about interaction on spaces like LiveJournal, things became clearer. In a sense, LiveJournal allows you to be either Narcissus or Echo. If you choose to turn off the comments feature, is possible to use the service as soapbox, devoted only to your declamations. Most people don't use LiveJournal in this way, though, and do allow comments. "I find I get more out of the comments when I look back through my journal than I do from my entries themselves," confesses LiveJournal user Trista:

> The comments bring memories back to me more vividly, a lot like a favorite perfume from ten years ago brings back memories of my job in the mall and the man I had a crush on. Reading those comments, the joking back and forth or the flirtiness or the offer of hugs and sympathy, takes me back to the time of the entry in a way that my paper journals have never done.[22]

In Chapter One, I explained the dialectical nature of Web communication, in which users offer their words and images to others, only to find themselves mirrored back in ways they don't expect. If the original user doesn't respond to these replies, she might indeed be engaging in a narcissistic practice. But if she responds, and others take her response as a charge to spread the dialogue outwards to their networks, we begin to enter the space of Echo, the repeater. Repetition—which involves both reflection and inflection—carries the possibility of change, as well as providing an ethical dimension to what was once pure narcissism.

The Case of ArtVamp

To demonstrate Spivak's argument, I want to share a story from the LiveJournal of ArtVamp. Formerly an escort, now an artist and pornographer, ArtVamp has long been something of a live wire in the camgirl community, infamous for her desire to be "sexually transgressive" in her relationship to her audience. None of that history, however, prepared me to find the following post in her journal:

Friday, August 23rd, 2002

11:13a - VISIT FROM THE FBI

Funny thing happened today.

I was walking 'round in my robe. Habibi [ArtVamp's husband; also a LiveJournal user] was getting ready to meet up with superstar filmmaker Shawn Durr to make dubs of one of his tapes. The doorbell downstairs rang, so Habibi thought it was Shawn and ran down stairs to greet him. He darted back up the stairs and said, "It's the F.B.I.!!!!"

"You're kidding right?" I said, knowing his sense of humor. The look on his face answered my question. He was half smiling, half astonished. "No," he said, "I am not."

I went into the bedroom to put some jeans on and from behind the door I listened to their conversation as they came up the stairs and into the apartment.

"Are you alone here?" an unfamiliar male voice asked.

"No, my wife is here," I heard Habibi say, possibly motioning to the bedroom.

"Actually, she's the one we want to talk to," said one of the agents.

I stopped. I searched my brain. Me? Why would they want to talk to me?! Habibi is the Arab boy! Wait, Internet porn *is* legal, right?!

Habibi expressed his surprise and spoke with them a little longer. I hastened to pull on a button up shirt, bypassing the bra and walked out. Two suited agents were standing in the kitchen. I was surprisingly not at all nervous. I mean, why should I be? I have nothing to hide. I was more amused than anything. Me! They want to talk to *me*!

We shook hands and sat down at the kitchen table. In the meantime, Shawn Durr showed up and made his way upstairs to witness my interrogation. I say interrogation, but really it was nothing like that at all. They were extremely friendly and following up on stupid hysterical anonymous tips is par for the course for them. They treated me with respect.

"You run a web site, correct?" One of the agents asked, looking through his papers, on which my social security number and various other stats are printed. "Art .... ."

"ArtVamp," I replied.

They explained that someone reported that I had written on my website (in this journal I presume) something about the next suicide bomber would be a white female because no one is expecting that. (Of course we all know it was [name omitted], don't we?)

They just wanted to make sure I didn't intend any violence—that I wasn't planning on being that white female suicide bomber. And as a matter of course, they had to ask whether I knew anyone who might be planning on committing any violent act against the U.S. or Israel.

Sheesh. How many times do I have to state clearly that I abhor violence for the idiot reactionaries out there to get it? I AM NOT VIOLENT! I DO NOT CONDONE VIOLENCE! VIOLENCE IS WRONG! Clear enough for you?

Anyway, except for being nearly naked when they showed up, it was not at all an unpleasant experience. The agents were super nice and polite. They took down my work address and phone number (Yes, sir, I do work in the Hancock—the second tallest building in Chicago. No sir, I have no plans nor any desire to blow it up.). Satisfied that I am just a girl with strong political opinions, they left.

They stressed that my and my Habibi's political views are not being questioned. We live in a free country and we are entitled by virtue of living here to express anything we damn-well please, just so long as we are not committing violent acts against anyone. It's called FREEDOM OF SPEECH y'all.

So THERE! We can say what we like, and you, you who think reporting us to the FBI will shut us up, can't do ANYTHING about it. Got it?! So fuck you!

Anyway, that was interesting. When they left Shawn was all impressed, 'cause he likes drama. He said he was proud, and so glad he got to see it. He wished he could have videotaped it. :) What a weird morning. The inevitable finally came to fruition, I'd say. You knew it was going to happen, didn't you?[23]

Politicizing the Personal

In the space of a day, thousands of LiveJournal users stopped by ArtVamp's site to read about and comment on her visit from the FBI. Many had never heard of her prior to this incident, but were linked to her story from other LiveJournal friends. On LiveJournal, a number of users counseled against getting overly panicked by this episode, when there were far worse tales of FBI abuse every day. As user Scott (known online as Whorlpool) put it, "I don't want folks thinking, 'Well if that is the worst going on, it's not all that bad, "frankly … 'and" then abandoning interest."[24]

I have difficulties with Scott's position for two reasons. First, although I certainly think detainment without attorney is more perilous than getting a visit from the FBI, I don't see one situation as more 'real' or significant than the other. I've seen this logic used in the queer community in extremely divisive ways—for example, in conversations where AIDS is considered a 'real issue,' but domestic violence among same-sex partners is not.

My second objection has to do with the nature of self-expression in today's political climate. ArtVamp was neither a high-profile political dissident nor someone likely to be profiled by the FBI. She was simply an American girl who happened to fall in love with an Iraqi expatriate. If a person with all ArtVamp's advantages of racial and economic privilege can't speak freely about this country's policies, I asked, do we honestly expect those with less social, economic, and political power to do so?

LiveJournal user Laura Fokkena agreed with me, putting a new spin on my notion of the grab when she observed, "Whenever you hear stories about the government-come-knocking, there's *always* this immediate oh-shit, welcome-to-my-life reaction that I find so fascinating." She continued:

> The activist who just put away the bong. ArtVamp in her robe. … Palestinians mention over and over again being in bed (i.e. a very private space) when the Israelis come into their homes. Aside from the bong, none of these things are illegal in and of themselves. And even the bong, well, it's a minor offense that only looms large when you're there to be arrested for something more sinister. But it's the reason even the most innocuous visit becomes An Event. I find myself frantically cleaning the house when I'd rather be doing other things, because who knows when the government is going to show up, asking me about my relationship to this or that Muslim, to this or that Arab?[25]

"Where I have REAL, probably-need-therapy-for-it ANGER," she continues, "is when people say that if you don't have connections to terrorism, you should brush off or even welcome such intrusions." Laura's comments remind us that the real problem with social capital is not its collapse, but rather its dispersal: in a networked environment, everyone is 'connected to terrorism,' if someone connects enough links between people.

Yet in a networked world, an organization like the FBI also creates as many relationships as it hopes to destroy. The day ArtVamp posted about her visit from the FBI, a huge number of LiveJournal users wound up instantly politicized, if only because something that we normally think of as happening to 'them' happened to 'us.' For those who rallied to her cause, ArtVamp served as a means for LiveJournal users to transition from a solipsistic preoccupation with ourselves to an ethical engagement with others.

Reflective Solidarity

In *Solidarity of Strangers,* Jodi Dean recalls a London *Times* report about a Somali woman giving birth on an Italian roadside where nobody stopped to help. Dean notes that the woman was alternately ignored or surveyed by passers-by. "as if they were at a cinema, careful not to miss the show."[26] When the story was made public through a local radio station, however, telephone calls supporting the woman began pouring in from across the Italian countryside. "What were callers seeking to get across with their expressions of solidarity?" asks Dean. "Why did they call at all?"[27]

Dean suggests two answers. First, the story roused the callers to shake off their numbness toward human suffering in general and reach out to a single human, letting her know that "what happened to her matters because she is a person whose integrity is like that of us all."[28] In addition, the Italians' offers of solidarity also reflected their belief that "concern for the welfare of another, an 'other' who is not Italian, was a constitutive part of their understanding of themselves as a group." Dean terms this move "reflective solidarity": a response to mediated suffering in which we choose to align ourselves politically with the other.

Andy Blunden emphasizes that true solidarity with another must be given on conditions determined by the recipient, not the giver. If the public sphere depends on discourse for its ethical structure (i.e., "the other person may be right, so I support them") and the counterpublic sphere depends on identity (i.e., "the other person may be *me,* so I support them"), reflective solidarity operates instead by acknowledging difference.[29] In reflective solidarity, I acknowledge that others are knowable to me only via conjecture or fantasy, yet I choose to believe in them and the affinity we share, and I vow to listen to them and support them.

Sometimes, though, we don't practice what we preach. In the fall of 2007, I was invited to speak at a law school conference devoted to privacy and the Web. I was happy to accept, especially when the conference organizers told me that the panel I was slated for was to be comprised entirely of feminist academics. Three months before the conference, I was informed that instead of speaking about our research, our panel was going to be organized as a "response roundtable." About a month before the conference, I was sent a DVD that contained a short movie, made by members of a cyberfeminism class at the law school, to which we would be asked to respond. We were also told that, in order to allow for audience input and participation, our response time was to be no more than five minutes each.

The video, while well-made, was theoretically underdeveloped. It seemed more like an "Introduction to Social Issues in Web 2.0" than anything else. As I watched, I wondered how I was expected to respond. Was I supposed to evaluate this as a piece of video, or as a critique of Web 2.0? Should I talk about the problematic framing of the camera's gaze throughout the piece, or attend to what the voice-over was saying? More crucially, what role was I supposed to play during the conference? Was I expected to interact as teacher, or as a colleague to the students?

Taking the coward's way out, I didn't raise these questions with the conference organizers, but instead started writing a response that helped push forward my own work on another paper I had due. From that paper, I extracted five minutes that critiqued a portion of the video, entertained the crowd, and made me look very clever. It also insulted the students and alienated the professor who had arranged for the DVD to be made.

Months later, I am till trying to put things together in my head, but I am starting to see how my frustration with the conference's set-up morphed into a piece of writing that attacked the very people I should have spent my time forging alliances with: the students. Although I stand by much of my critique of the video, I now regret the manner in which I said what I did. I intended my thoughts to work as a first salvo in a dialogue with the students, but as anyone who has ever attended an academic conference knows, power rests with those on the podium, no matter how much time is left for audience participation.

Even as I write this, though, I have to admit to myself that my rationalizations are bollocks, as they say in England. I am the one brought to conferences to be an 'internet person': I am the one who writes about tele-ethicality. I'm always banging on about how Web 2.0 allows many-to-many communication. Why should I blame the organizers for not putting me in touch with the students (they were busy planning a conference), when a quick mail to them would have given me the contact information for every student making the video? It's not like I haven't launched a million blogs in the past, some of them password-protected, even. We could have laid all sorts of groundwork together weeks before this conference, if someone (read: me) had prepared beforehand.

In hindsight, here is what I should have done if I really wanted to speak with the students: I should have initiated—and, if necessary, technologically facilitated—dialogue prior to the conference. I should have demonstrated trustworthy behavior, instead of denying my own position of power as the unopposed speaker on stage. I should have made it plain that even if I didn't agree with some of the representational strategies of the video, my assumption was that we were on allied 'teams' with similar end goals. In my head I was thinking, "I wouldn't critique this so harshly if I didn't think you could push your thinking more," but now I realize this is about as useful as a Little League Dad who yells at his kid to run faster. A little appreciation goes a long way in a critique, and I was awfully stingy with mine.

In short: if solidarity was what I came for, I had a funny way of showing it. And I *was* after solidarity. I'm not saying these things to assuage my conscience. I'm saying it because I believe more in micro than in macro politics. No point in waiting for Live Aid to save the day if we can't muster up the effort to forge connections with the dozen or so people who actually *want* to talk with us—even (especially) when those people strike us as missing the point, or as wrong-headed in their views.

My failure that day, and the fact that no students wanted to answer my follow-up email to the conference attendees, led me to arrive at three 'rules' regarding the formation of networked reflective solidarity. First, I have come to realize that even in professional circles, people will always rely on the opinions of 'friends' over experts. I place scare quotes around this term to indicate that I am again thinking of friend as a catachresis, rather than as an essential category. Had I approached the students by extending online friendship in addition to offline expertise, there is a chance I would have had more success at the conference.

Second, I now understand that networked reflective solidarity only works among those who perceive themselves to be part of a relational, rather than universal, public. Had I stopped writing my law school talk for a generic audience and actually discovered the motives of the students making the video, I would be communicating productively with them today.

Finally, it is necessary to appreciate one's mistakes as well as victories. Misunderstanding, miscommunication, and uncertainty are part and parcel of networked reflective solidarity. The commitment is not to eradicate these challenges, but rather to press on despite them.

Discovering Anjum

I don't think I will ever forget how I discovered Anjum's LiveJournal: It was not long after the events of September 11, 2001.[30] I was living in New York, writing in my journal as a way to process the political unrest of the moment. For my trouble, I received a large quantity of hostile email from readers of my journal who thought my political views were "dangerously liberal." One night over drinks, I whined to a friend about the way I was being harassed online for speaking my mind, only to have him respond, "Wow. That's rough. How are Arab and Arab-American LiveJournal users dealing with all this hostility?"

It was only then that I realized that I wasn't reading any journals by Arabs or Arab Americans—at the time, my LiveJournal Friends List consisted mainly of people in webcamming communities and people who had added me to their lists first. Embarrassed that I simply didn't know many "real live Arabs" with LiveJournals, I began searching for them. First, I looked up people who had keywords in their interest lists such as "Islam," "Arabic," "intifada," "Palestine," and "postcolonial." I also spent a great deal of time looking through the Friends Lists of people such as Usama Alshaibi, who is ArtVamp's husband "Habibi," mentioned above. Alshaibi, born in Baghdad in 1969 and educated in the United States, currently works as an avant-garde filmmaker, which is how he met ArtVamp. He is routinely outspoken about political issues in his journal—far more so than ArtVamp—which explains her musing above that the FBI must be interested in him and not her.

A cynic would rightly point out that I was on a bit of an orientalist treasure hunt, actively seeking out new friends solely on the basis of what I perceived as their exotic origin. Treasure hunting is cause for legitimate concern, not least because the practice resembles the commodity fetishism of social capital discussed earlier. Kevin Barbieux's "Homeless Guy" podcast (complete with "Homeless Guy" theme song) has many subscribers, yet despite his popularity, "shelter in Nashville, Tennessee" remains on his Wish List.[31] Until social capital puts a roof over Kevin's head, this is a problem that needs addressing.

My friend Kim likes to say that sometimes it is okay to do the right thing for the wrong reasons. I think about her counsel every time I see a LiveJournal post from Anjum, a student at Syracuse University. I first 'met' Anjum while reading through her very personal thoughts regarding her decision to stop wearing *hijab*, and her frustration with other people's readings of her decision as being about either "sexual freedom" or "turning her back on the Koran." Through her journal, Anjum showed me that her decision to not wear *hijab* (and it is not a permanent decision, but a shifting one) reflected an engagement with her faith, rather than an abandonment of it.

My continued LiveJournal friendship with Anjum runs counter to the 'Arab woman as problem' narrative shown on television every night. I could have seen a story similar to Anjum's on the Public Broadcasting Network. The difference is that I don't correspond with people I see on PBS, I don't keep up with their quotidian activities, I don't offer to write them graduate school recommendations, and I don't make plans to meet them offline. I don't think of them as friends.

With friendship comes the responsibility to face two contradictory yet coexistent ideologies regarding online networks. One view holds that the Web can and should provide a safe harbor for those seeking compassion and support. The story of my trip from my mother's hospital room to Echo is an example of this view. The other position is that anything said on the Web is public knowledge. This means that sometimes a simple nod to someone's existence—whether to scapegoat or to celebrate—makes them vulnerable. Laura Fokkena, who has social ties with a number of 'illegal aliens' explains:

> There are so many political points I'd like to make when I write (online or in print) but attracting attention to myself might mean attracting attention to others. How could I live with myself if something I just dashed off on the Internet ended up getting someone else in very real trouble? And yet, how could I live with myself if I said nothing?[32]

How Could I Live With Myself?

How could I live with myself if I said nothing? In an essay titled "Our Sisters from Stable Countries," Canadian law professor Audrey Macklin relates her time spent working for a Canadian oil company doing business in Southern Sudan, a country whose decades-long civil war has been long subsidized by oil interests.[33] Macklin was sent along with a team of attorneys to investigate whether contacts of the oil company in question were directly involved in any human rights abuses in the area. In a meeting with internal refugees, a woman addressed Macklin and her two female colleagues with the words "Greetings, sisters … We thank God he has brought women to see our problems. … We are happy today to see women and men together as equal people in the world. … If women have come to interview us, we know women are equal."[34]

"At first," confessed Macklin, "the [women refugees'] reference to sisterhood and equality left me deeply uncomfortable, almost embarrassed."[35] She notes that rather than sisters, the Sudanese women could have addressed them as corporate apologists, as Westerners, as white women, or "as the beneficiaries of oil stolen from their land and over their dead bodies."[36] Macklin admits her next reaction was the arrogant feminist presumption "I guess they haven't heard about [critiques of] essentialism."[37] On further reflection, however, she realized that when such a woman greeted her "as a sister, the work done by sisterhood is not the same as if I had been the one to invoke it."[38] Her use of the word "sister" worked catachrestically, in other words, in the same way as the LiveJournal term "friend."

Macklin concludes her essay by arguing that the Sudanese invocation of "sister" constituted a challenge to First World women to combine "detachment with relationship, pity with accountability and confrontation with engagement."[39] I see this story as a great example of networked reflective solidarity. Here, the network accessed by the Sudanese women wasn't the Internet, but rather the network of international human rights workers sent by Big Oil. The Sudanese women demonstrated how the availability of a network—any network—can be the beginning of change, under one vital condition: those receiving the transmission must understand that, in Macklin's words, "I *am* my sister's keeper. And she is my keeper."[40]

In a follow-up postscript to her original essay, Macklin informs her readers that the women she met in Sudan are now dead, caught in the violence they were desperately trying to tell the world about—violence fueled in part by her country's need for gasoline. In that moment I understood why Macklin wrote her story: to hail her readers as sisters, the way she had been hailed. Our mutual engagement began in the networks of multinational corporations and global human rights organizations, but surely it cannot end with my downloading her story over the Web and reading it in my bedroom, alone in New York. Surely, I am somehow responsible for continuing the connection. When we as feminists enter into networked space (which today is nearly all space), we must understand that at any moment we may find ourselves hailed as a friend, as a sister. And once we are, how can we live with ourselves if we do nothing?

Conclusion:
Moving From 'Sisters' to Sisters

Dear Ms. Senft,

Please stop cluttering up perfectly good cyberspace with your self-indulgent drivel and study something of use. Better yet, why don't you commit yourself to real feminism? Volunteer some time in a battered women's shelter. Teach English as a second language to a woman who needs that skill to get a job. Your brand of chic, poetic feminism is an embarrassment to the women who fought so diligently for you in the 1960's and 70's. You should be ashamed.

Oh, I almost forgot! Do you wanna cyber sometime? You are such a hottie!

Sincerely

XXXXX

I began this book by asking what it means for feminists to speak of the personal as political in the age of networks. I'd like to end by recapping some of my ongoing fears, encapsulated nicely enough by an actual piece of hate mail I received in 2001. This project has spanned nearly eight years of research, writing, and revision, and in that time, I've had lots of opportunities to question the value of what we've all been doing online. For better or worse, I'm still a believer.

From Lawrence Lessig: "A time is marked not so much by ideas that are argued about but ideas that are taken for granted."[1] The argument of this book has been that most of our ideas about the personal and the political in network society derive from mistaken beliefs about our world that we take for granted. These beliefs are entangled with our understandings of publicity, commodity, epistemology, pornography, and social capital. In each chapter of this book, I have explored the ways camgirls and social network users have responded to these lures, so that those of us interested in a progressive ethics might learn from their experiences.

In Chapter One, I considered the ideology of publicity: the belief that what matters is what is known. I detailed how camgirls employ theatrical authenticity, self-branding and celebrity as forms of publicity. I then explained how micro-celebrity destabilizes ideologies of publicity by emphasizing responsiveness to, rather than distancing from, one's community. Rather than obsessing over what micro-celebrities are 'really' like, viewers deal with them in real time, focused on real issues, with real chances for human contact. Later, in Chapter Five, I showed how this sense of connection and obligation sometimes creates a space for networked reflective solidarity: a political identification that simultaneously hails the viewer/listener as 'one of us' and insists that one cannot know everything about anyone, all the time.

In Chapter Two, I addressed the ideology of commodity: the belief that what matters is what can be owned. This is clearly seen in the Web's aesthetic of the grab, which differs from the voyeuristic gaze of film in that it allows viewers to take what they want and rework or discard the rest. As expert manipulators of the grab, camgirls often present themselves as branded commodities to be consumed. Yet when an audience grabs her in ways she does not anticipate or desire, the camgirl comes to understand that however much she brands herself as product, she is ultimately a woman engaged in a particular type of emotional labor.

An ancillary task of this book has been to update Donna Haraway's 1984 figure of the cyborg to better reflect the concerns of feminists in the early twenty-first century. Haraway's "Manifesto for Cyborgs" was first and foremost an attack on notions of essential womanhood derived through biological imperative, and the metaphor of the cyborg was originally intended to generate feelings of affinity among connected parties.[2] In Chapter Two, I argued that camgirls can help feminists understand the complexities of what we might think of as the First World's forgotten cyborgs: nannies, home companions, and sex workers in the 'caring' sectors of our economies.

In Chapter Three, I considered the ideology of epistemology: the belief that the truth is out there, if only we take the time to uncover it. I argued that society is in trouble when we use this ideology to forestall ethical action in mediated environments, because in a world saturated by information, that moment of full understanding never arrives. As a remedy, I advocated tele-ethicality: a commitment to engage, rather than forestall action in our mediated communities, despite the potential for fakery and fraud. I argued that tele-ethicality not only aids action in mediated environments, but also helps us better understand the ways in which we create virtualized cyborgs: bodies whose concerns we render unreal via media, such as women whose lives we eagerly consume in our books and broadcasts, but whom we often dismiss as 'crazy' in our everyday lives.

Chapter Four analyzed the ideology of the pornographic: the belief that specific, feminized bodies ought to be scapegoats for shifting relationships between public and private in a culture. Building on Lauren Berlant's argument that ours is the time of the intimate public sphere (in which a preoccupation with sexual display substitutes for engagement with political issues of the day), I suggested that camgirls are this moment's 'pornographized cyborgs': bodies whose existence is deemed prurient simply because they exist on camera.[3] I asked whether camgirl-inspired porn might work as a form of camp resistance to a contemporary obsession with prurience over politics. I concluded that it cannot, in part because the Web doesn't work in the same way as the counterpublic areas in which camp traditionally occurs. Rather than a series of discrete spheres, the Web is better thought of as a series of networked, quasi-public spaces peopled by both familiar strangers and strange familiars. In such an environment, the private, the public, and the pornographic will always be a relational, rather than universal, affair.

In Chapter Five, I examined the ideology of social capital: the belief that human relationships can be quantified, managed, controlled, and hoarded as if they were material goods. I argued that although the desire to protect one's community from untrustworthy outsiders is understandable, we cannot afford to forestall action in our networks until appropriate levels of social capital have been aggregated by those we do not know. Instead, we must use our networks to locate and engage with others through what I have described as networked reflective solidarity. In making trust a matter of ethical choice rather than social capital, we admit the possibility of deceit, fraud, and plain misunderstanding on both sides, yet we press on.

I want to end this book with five recommendations to feminists seeking to make the personal political in the time of global media. Many of these recommendations turn on the work of Michael Apple, who has spent the past decade analyzing the rise of political and religious conservatives in America, and suggesting ways to interrupt their power base.[4] My recommendations for feminists in the time of networks are as follows: emphasize the cultural, respect the locals and the strangers, think heretically, take ethical action and seek solidarity with friends and 'friends.'

Emphasize the Cultural

In Chapter Two, I asked why there was a phenomenon known as 'camgirls,' yet no analogous phenomenon of 'camguys' outside of gay subculture. In Chapter Five, I asked why commentators have written so much about the political value of filter blogs linked to news sources, yet have virtually ignored the political value of personal blogs such as LiveJournal. In both cases, the answer I have received in the past is "That's just how the world works." Feminists and other progressives need to view this response as a cue to begin conversations on these issues, not to end them.

One way to reassert the political importance of the personal is to move away from a preoccupation with *why* something is so, toward a more rigorous analysis of *how* certain behaviors network into a naturalized version of "the way it is." In Chapter Four, I demonstrated that a preoccupation with the question of why there are female exhibitionists online distracts us from understanding how all Web users exist in an *x* degrees of separation relationship to the sex industry. Similarly, allowing pundits to remain locked in discussions of why ours is a time of voyeur nations, celebrity cultures, and 'postfeminisms' obscures how some forms of expression come to be seen as political, whereas others remain in the ghetto of the personal, and how women's bodies have come to account for a disproportionate number of our forgotten, virtualized, and pornographized cyborgs.

Respect the Locals and the Strangers

In Chapter Five, I pointed out that Web users are faced with two narratives regarding life online. In the first, the Web is the last hope for a public sphere, which explains why it is almost impossible to object to a line of discussion anywhere without someone chiming in about the right to free speech. In the second, the Web is a danger zone, full of hostility, as evidenced by the letter from the reader who thought I was insulting feminism with my work. Although it is understandable that Web users desire a safe space for their expression, it is important to see how our desire to survey, screen, filter, measure, and control online replicates a larger cultural impulse to spy, limit access, profile, redline, quota, and otherwise discipline individuals, neighborhoods, and countries we perceive as an *a priori* threat to our well-being.

After I received the note from the hostile reader, I chose not to hide it, but instead posted it to my LiveJournal. While I received many heartening responses, my favorite came from my friend Amber. "This 'women shouldn't think about cultural studies when there are real problems' stuff is the sort of thing that makes me mental," wrote Amber, who was working at a battered women's shelter. She continued:

> People need to stop this disconnect between on-the-ground activism and the rest of life. I don't have the time to explain to the folks donating "special makeover days" for the women in our place that I feel deeply conflicted and ambivalent about their help. I don't even know HOW to explain that. That's not what we do with our day jobs, but it is what you do. Speaking as someone who does 'real' feminist work, I need people like you out there. *We* need you.[5]

In 2001, after receiving Amber's note, I placed the following post on my LiveJournal:

> I'm going to keep writing stuff for public consumption because well, that's my job. In my heady moments, I think of myself (and many of you) as public intellectuals in training. To me, a public intellectual is someone who tries to keep rationality and compassion going, especially in irrational and dispassionate times. She is someone who takes things so much to heart that she commits herself to not taking other people's rage (or praise) personally. And more to the point, she is someone strong enough to resist when attacked. Rather than launching a counter-strike, she throws some dirt on her injuries and walks them off. Because, in a very important sense, she asked for it.

In 2007, six years after announcing I would take the force of any intellectual blow delivered my way, I turned to the LiveJournal community to get their help resisting a different kind of violence. Here is the post I made to the Friends Only section of my journal, under the heading, "Semi-public declaration, because I need to be kept honest about this":

> For the last year of my life, I have been in a relationship that, while lovely at times, has largely been marked by abuse, both mental and physical. I never thought I would be 'that person,' I never thought I would be the one left by an abusive man, and I never thought I would be sad about losing him.

> I've been largely silent about all this, because who wants to admit to it, you know? A few months ago, a friend told me I was exhibiting symptoms that seemed dangerously close to Stockholm syndrome. I have difficulty being publicly angry at the way I've been treated because I can already hear my ex's voice in my head, accusing me of 'running to my friends' and 'not understanding that things are hard for him, too.'

> A week ago, he broke things off with me, but still 'really wants a close friendship.' I'm not sure what this could possibly mean, since I've never had a friend speak to me like I was garbage, mock things that were important to me, or hit me (and he denies this happened in the way I experienced it, because that's what he does).

> What I need to do is cut him out of my life completely. This is hard, because I live in a city where my normal network of friends and family isn't around. I'm pretty nervous about this, not least because I'm not drinking or doing anything I would normally do to dull the ache of everything. I cannot believe I threw away a year of my life trying to save something that cannot be saved.

> So I want to make a public declaration (at least to my friends list):

> I'm not contacting this person anymore. I've eliminated all his phone numbers and chat icons from all my devices. I'm leaving for two weeks to the States and Canada on conferences, so I'll be distracted. I need to stop hiding all this, because it's not serving me to fall apart, and then have him show back up when he feels lonely or contrite, and then start all this over again. I am tired of being an Oprah episode.

> Repeat: I never thought I would be writing something like this. I really didn't.

At the beginning of this book, I endorsed Gayatri Spivak's claim that ethics requires us to stay long enough to listen to what others have to say, especially when what they're saying strikes us as irrational, backward, or at odds with what we perceive to be their best interests. Networked reflective solidarity likewise requires not just that we take it upon ourselves to cross borders, but that we curb our instinctive desire to protect ourselves when we feel our own borders have been crossed by strangers.

Sometimes this business of opening and closing borders takes some negotiation. I chose to make my admission Friends Only, but I have a Friends List that is more than 500 people. The people I didn't want to see my words—my current students, my employers, my family—did not see them, although of course someone could have breached my confidence during that time. (Clearly, I no longer worry about who sees what with regard to this incident.)

In addition to people I've never met before, there are people like my best friend who knew of my situation, but to whom I hadn't communicated about it in writing. For a writer, this is a big issue. By putting my thoughts online (and asking for help keeping my commitment) I wanted to communicate to my best friend that she didn't have to shoulder the entire burden of caring for me during a difficult time. And I was supported. Later I found out about the elaborate back-channel my online friends had developed between themselves—consisting of instant messages, texts and phone calls to one another—so they could assure themselves that someone was caring for me at all times. Thinking of it today still makes me weep with appreciation.

Think Heretically and Take Ethical Action

My third recommendation for feminists in the time of networks is to think heretically about some of our most dearly held beliefs, particularly regarding sex work and young people's sexuality, ideally taking our cue regarding appropriate lines of dialogue from children and sex workers themselves. I am not advocating preteen sexual activity. Nor do I champion the 'sex positive' notion that all sexual work under any conditions is liberating, so long as I choose it for myself. I am simply urging a relational, individual, and local approach to these issues, rather than the current universal, abstract, and global dictates exemplified by the Bush administration.

In essence, I am talking about ethics through micropolitics. In this book I have urged feminists to consider the power of local conversations and actions in nonpolitical arenas like the dinner table, the movies, or on the Web. Like William Connolly, I believe that micropolitics "sets the stage for macro politics by rendering people receptive or unreceptive to certain messages and plans of action."[6] On the Web, micropolitical tele-ethical acts might include, among other things, online dialogues, building communities, 'outing' oneself online, and even intervening when someone's safety is at stake, as in my own story.

Curiously, among the most powerful things about tele-ethicality is that it does not require co-presence to work and often functions more effectively when parties are at a physical remove from one another. There is nobody closer to me than my brothers, but I could not talk about my abusive relationship with them, in part because I felt it to be a repetition of my mother's history with my father. I was too ashamed to go to a battered women's group, since I had always considered myself the type of woman who works at a shelter, not the kind who needs one (it's hard to feel *noblesse oblige* toward 'poor others' when you have a black eye yourself.) I couldn't talk to anyone at work because I was concerned that I would be taken less seriously as a feminist scholar (it turned out I was wrong on this count, but that was my feeling at the time). The place I turned—the only place I felt I *could* turn, given the trauma my revelations would cause loved ones far from me at the time—was LiveJournal, the very place I had started off with my webcam in the early days of 2000.

Seek Solidarity with Both Friends and 'Friends'

In the past eight years, I have come to learn that networked reflective solidarity requires both friends and 'friends,' to use the LiveJournal parlance. I am not saying we should gloss over differences between the two for the sake of connection, but that we should remain focused on our aim in solidarity. For feminists, making the personal political in the time of networks will mean locating friendships in both familiar and strange places, making a concerted effort to reach out beyond our psychic borders, and remaining open to others who do the same. When we begin to understand friendship as contingent and subject to change, we may begin to see that antagonism too is a relational, rather than permanent, state of affairs.

Notes

Introduction

1. danah boyd and Nicole Ellison define social networking systems as "web-based services that allow individuals to (1) construct a public or semi-public profile within a bounded system, (2) articulate a list of other users with whom they share a connection, and (3) view and traverse their list of connections and those made by others within the system. The nature and nomenclature of these connections may vary from site to site." See danah boyd and Nicole Ellison, "Social network sites: Definition, history, and scholarship," *Journal of Computer-Mediated Communication* 13.1 (2007). Online at http://jcmc.indiana.edu/vol13/issue1/boyd.ellison.html (viewed March 3, 2008). YouTubecan be reached at http://www.youtube.com. MySpace is at http://www.myspace.com, and Facebook at http://www.facebook.com.

2. I use the term 'viewer' because it is part of the camgirl vernacular, though it will become obvious soon enough that many of the people entering into these communities are far from passive recipients of the events transpiring on their screens.

3. The Terricam was available on a regular basis from 2000–2002, and is now only live for special occasions like the broadcast of my Ph.D. dissertation defense in 2004. See http://www.terrisenft.net/webcam/Terricam.html (viewed August 6, 2006). Each time I discuss a camgirl in this book, I provide a footnote detailing the status of her site to date.

4. LiveJournal is located at http://www.livejournal.com My LiveJournal is at http://www.livejournal.com/users/tsenft.

5. "How to start your own consciousness-raising group." The article was originally a Chicago Women's Liberation Union leaflet, and was reprinted in *Black Maria* magazine in 1971. Available online at http://www.cwluherstory.org/consciousness/how-to-start-your-own-consciousness-raising-group-2.html.

6. Carol Hanisch, "The Personal Is Political" in *Notes from the Second Year: Women's Liberation,* Eds. Shulamith Firestone and Anne Koedt (New York: Firestone and Koedt, 1970), 204–205.

7. Carol Hanisch, "Updated Introduction to the Personal is Political." Alexander Street Press *Second Wave and Beyond* website, Online at http://scholar.alexanderstreet.com/pages/viewpage.action?pageId=2259 (viewed July 1, 2006).

8. For a historical overview of the events in music leading to the Riot Grrl movement, see Maria Raha, *Cinderella's Big Score: Women of the Punk and Indie Underground* (Emeryville: Seal Press, 2004).

9. For more on women and zine's, see Stephen Duncombe, *Notes from Underground: Zine's and the Politics of Alternative Culture* (New York: Verso, 1997).

10. Rita Felski, *Beyond Feminist Aesthetics: Feminist Literature and Social Change* (Cambridge, MA: Harvard University Press, 1989), 86.

11. Walter Benjamin, "The Work of Art in the Age of Mechanical Reproduction," in *Illumination* (New York: Schocken, 1968), 219.

12. Robert Hughes, *The Shock of The New: Art and the Century of Change* (London: Thames & Hudson, 1991).

13. Because its membership is spread around the globe, LiveJournal differs from older geographically-bound virtual communities like The WELL or Echo in that users don't have regularly scheduled live meetings with one another. That said, members in certain areas do get together on an impromptu basis from time to time, and it was at those meetings where I met some of my research subjects.

14. See Harry Kreisler, "Conversation with Manuel Castells, p. 4 of 6." *Conversations with History; Institute of International Studies,* UC Berkeley. Available online at http://globetrotter.berkeley.edu/people/Castells/castells-con4.html (viewed 8 August 2006). See also Manuel Castells, *The Rise of the Network Society* (Cambridge, MA: Blackwell, 1996). For their overview of Castells, I am indebted to William Davies and James Crabtree, "Invisible Villages: Technolocalism and Community Renewal," *Renewal: A Journal of Labour Politics* 12.1 (2004). Available online at http://www.renewal.org.uk/issues/2004%20Voulme%2012/Invisible%20Villages.htm (viewed August 6, 2006).

15. Kreisler, "Conversation With Manuel Castells."

16. Castells, *Rise of the Network Society.*

17. Jodi Dean, "Feminism in Technoculture." Keynote Address: Feminist Millennium Conference, University of Bergen, Norway, April 27–29, 2000. Available online at http://people.hws.edu/dean/fem_tech.html (viewed August 6, 2006).

18. See Chandra Mohanty, "'Under Western Eyes' Revisited: Feminist Solidarity through Anticapitalist Struggles," *Signs* 28.2 (2003): 511.

19. See Evelyn Hu-DeHart, "Globalization and Its Discontents: Exposing the Underside," *Frontiers: A Journal of Women Studies* 24.2 (2004): 252.

20. Kamala Kempadoo, "Introduction: Globalizing Sex Workers' Rights," in *Global Sex Workers: Rights, Resistance, and Redefinition,* eds. Kamala Kempadoo and Jo Dozema (New York: Routledge, 1998), 28.

21. Dean, "Feminism in Technoculture."

22. Andrew Calcutt, "Myths and Realities of the Digital Divide." No date provided. *Internet Freedom Blog.* Available online at http://www.netfreedom.org/controversy/latest/calcutt.asp (viewed August 28, 2006).

23. Jodi Dean, *Publicity's Secret: How Technoculture Capitalizes on Democracy* (Ithaca, NY: Cornell University Press, 2002), 129.

24. Oddly, I was unable to locate camgirls in South Korea, a country with legendary broadband penetration, an interest in celebrity culture and no particular prohibitions against female self-expression.

25. Anabella's AnabellaCam site, live since 1998, is available online at http://www.anabella.com.ar/ (viewed August 28, 2006).

26. Although some communities of camgirls were left out of my research by design, others I was unable to locate despite multiple attempts. For example, although I knew

African American women are a fast-growing sector of Internet users, I had difficulty finding nonwhite camgirls to interview for this project. According to Pew Internet Research, English-speaking Asian Americans rank among the highest in Internet use, at 75 percent or 5 million members. White adults follow them at 58 percent, English-speaking Hispanics at 50 percent, and African Americans at 43 percent. See "Asian Americans and the Internet: The Young and Connected." Available online at http://www.pewinternet.org/reports/reports.asp?Report=52&Section=ReportLevel 2&Field=Level2ID&ID=345 (viewed August 28, 2006). Only one non-white camgirl—Auriea Harvey—repeatedly appears in this book, and as an expatriate African American artist living and working in Belgium, Auriea can hardly be said to be representative of any community's experience. Auriea Harvey's Web site is available online at http://e8z.org (viewed August 28, 2006).

27. The Wayback Machine is at http://www.archive.org
28. Unlike today, when any search for 'dissertation' and 'webcam' yields a couple of dozen people writing on the subject, back then I was a rarity. Although I never formally tracked Web traffic, I think my popularity reached its peak around the time I was appearing in Aerlyn Weissman's documentary film *Webcam Girls*, which appeared on Canadian television.
29. Jennifer's JenniCam, which existed from 1996 to 2004, was available online at http://www.jennicam.org (viewed December 30, 2003). Ana Voog's AnaCam, which began in 1997, is located at http://www.AnaCam.com (viewed August 28, 2006).
30. The link came by way of a story published by the now-defunct *Lingua Franca*, which was a sort of *People* magazine of U.S. academia. See Scott MacLemme, "I am a Camera," *Lingua Franca*, January 2001. Online at http://www.mclemee.com/id36.html (viewed September 1, 2007).
31. Arlie Russell Hochschild, *The Managed Heart: Commercialization of Human Feeling* (Berkeley, CA: University of California Press, 1983). For a review of Hoschild and other theorists of emotional labor, see Alicia A. Grandey, "Emotion in the Workplace: A New Way to Conceptualize Emotional Labor," *Journal of Occupational Health Psychology* 5.1 (2000): 95–110.
32. Hochschild quoted in Grandey, "Emotion in the Workplace," 96.
33. Email interview with the author, October 8, 2001.
34. Email interview with the author, August 22, 2001.
35. Interview with the author, March 11, 2001. Alan maintains a LiveJournal, but asked that I not disclose its URL in this book.
36. Interview with the author, November 10, 2001. Frank keeps a LiveJournal at http://www.livejournal.com/users/grass (viewed August 28, 2006).
37. Email interview with the author, September 3, 2001. Scott's LiveJournal is available at http://www.livejournal.com/users/whorlpool (viewed September 19, 2003).
38. Email interview with the author, August 4, 2001. HereandNow was online from 1998 to 2002 at http://www.hereandnow.net (viewed October 7, 2001).
39. Email interview with the author, August 17, 2001. Melissa Gira's "Beautiful Toxin" site, online since 2000, has moved to "Sacred Whore" at http://www.melissagira.com (viewed August 28, 2006). Melissa also maintains the "Sexerati" blog at http://www.sexerati.com (viewed August 1, 2007).
40. P. David Marshall, *Celebrity and Power: Fame in Contemporary Culture* (Minneapolis: University of Minnesota Press, 1997), 17.
41. Viewers can still watch the CornCam at http://www.iowafarmer.com/corn_cam/ (viewed August 28, 2006).

42. The Web site for the South by Southwest Conference is at http://www.sxsw.com/ (viewed August 28, 2006).

43. HereandNow was online from 1998 to 2002 at http://www.hereandnow.net (viewed October 7, 2001). Lisa Batey currently maintains a LiveJournal at http://www.live-journal.com/users/lisagoddess and is broadcasting from Justin.tv under the name Nikomimi Lisa, at http://www.justin.tv.Andrea Mignolo no longer maintains a web presence.

44. It is important to understand that the number of journals created is greater than the number of individual users, since it is common for LiveJournal users to have multiple concurrent or consecutive accounts on the system. See the LiveJournal "Stats" site at http://www.livejournal.com/stats.bml (last viewed August 28, 2006).

45. Maarten Hajer and Hendrik Wagenaar, *Deliberative Policy Analysis: Understanding Governance in the Network Society* (Cambridge, U.K.: Cambridge University Press, 2003), 14–16.

46. See Gavin Poynter, "Emotions in the Labour Process," *European Journal of Psychotherapy, Counselling & Health* 5.3 (2002). Laura M. Agustin, "A Migrant World of Services," *Social Politics: International Studies in Gender, State and Society* 10.3 (2004), Heather Montgomery, "Children, Prostitution and Identity: A Case Study from a Tourist Resort in Thailand," in *Global Sex Workers: Right and Resistance, and Redefinition*, eds. Kamala Kempadoo and Jo Dozema (New York: Routledge, 1998), 139–150.

47. Kiva is at http://www.kiva.org; Facebook is at http://www.facebook.com.

48. Gayatri Chakravorty Spivak and Ellen Rooney, "In a Word: Interview," *Differences* 1.2 (1989): 124.

Chapter 1

1. Jennifer Ringley's JenniCam, which existed from 1996 to 2004, was available online at http://www.jennicam.org (viewed August 22, 2003).

2. Simon Firth, "Live! From My Bedroom!" *Salon*, January 8, 1998. Available online at http://archive.salon.com/21st/feature/1998/01/cov_08feature.html (viewed August 22, 2006).

3. See Museum of Modern Art, "Fame after Photography, July 8–October 5, 1999." Available online at http://www.moma.org/exhibitions/1999/fameafterphotography/ (viewed August 6, 2006).

4. Quentin Stafford-Fraser, "The Trojan Coffee Pot Timeline." Available online at http://www.cl.cam.ac.uk/coffee/qsf/timeline.html (viewed August 6, 2006).

5. Lynn M. Voskuil, "Feeling Public: Sensation Theater, Commodity Culture, and the Victorian Public Sphere," *Victorian Studies* 44.2 (2002): 245.

6. Christine Humphries, "Inside the Mind (and Bedroom) of a Web Star," ABCNews.com, April 22, 1998. Available online at http://abcnews.go.com/sections/tech/DailyNews/jennicam980422.html (viewed February 21, 2001).

7. Every so often, someone will link homecamming to discussions of the 'hyperreal,' a term coined by Umberto Eco in to describe our increased reliance on technological mediation to live our everyday lives. Those who remember *The Matrix* will recall the scene in which Morpheus welcomes Neo to the "desert of the real," after Neo flees from the Matrix. The quote comes from Jean Baudrillard, who argues that we now live in a *Matrix*-like environment dominated by simulations, rather than reality.

Unfortunately, the concept of hyperreality covers up as much as it makes clear. We know there is a difference between the hyperreal experience of watching a homecam and seeing images of a war in a far off country up-close through network television, but it's difficult to get at what that difference is through the language of the hyperreal. See Umberto Eco, *Travels in Hyperreality* (New York: Harcourt Press, 1990), and Jean Baudrillard, *Simulations, Semiotext(E) Foreign Agents Series* (New York: Semiotext(e) Inc., 1983).

8. IRC conversation with Jodi Anderson, business manager for Jennifer Ringley, October 22, 2001.

9. Interview with the author. Anabella's AnabellaCam site, live since 1998, is available online at http://www.anabella.com.ar/ (viewed August 28, 2006).

10. IRC conversation with Jodi Anderson, business manager for Jennifer Ringley, October 22, 2001.

11. Amandacam existed from 1998 to 2003 at http://www.amandacam.com (viewed November 22, 2002).

12. I do not intend to suggest here that camgirls were the only subculture present on LiveJournal at its inception—social networking services are spaces that can accommodate divergent subcultures simultaneously, and my claims about LiveJournal's place in camgirl subculture should not be taken as a suggestion that there were not other communities making their own use of the space at the time. Researcher danah boyd notes that when people first joined the social networking service Friendster, "three specific subcultures dominated the early adopters—bloggers, attendees of the Burning Man festival, and gay men mostly living in New York. ... Burners believed that the site was for Burners, gay men thought it was a gay dating site, and bloggers were ecstatic to have a geek socializing tool." The story is worth remembering when reading my impressions of LiveJournal via my experiences in camgirl communities. See danah boyd. "Friends, friendsters, and Top 8: Writing community into being on social network sites," *First Monday* 11.12 (December 2006). Online at http://firstmonday. org/issues/issue11_12/boyd/index.html.

13. Sherry Turkle, *The Second Self: Computers and the Human Spirit* (New York: Simon & Schuster, 1984).

14. Sherry Turkle, *Life on the Screen: Identity in the Age of the Internet* (New York: Simon & Schuster, 1995).

15. Email communication with the author, June 18, 2003. Alby has asked that the location of his LiveJournal remain private.

16. Email communication with the author, June 20, 2003. Scribble's LiveJournal is located at http://www.livejournal.com/users/scribble (viewed August 15, 2006).

17. Email communication with the author, July 7, 2003. Mia's LiveJournal is located at http://www.livejournal.com/users/nihilistech (viewed June 19, 2006).

18. Email communication with the author, July 5, 2003. Laura's LiveJournal is located at http://www.livejournal.com/users/slit (viewed June 19, 2006).

19. Email correspondence with the author, July 6, 2003. Helena has asked that her LiveJournal address be kept private.

20. Ibid.

21. For more information, see http://www.livejournal.com/support/faqbrowse. bml?faqid=61.

22. See danah boyd, "Friends, friendsters, and Top 8. Writing community into being on social network sites," *First Monday* 11.12 (December 2006). Online at http://first-monday.org/issues/issue11_12/boyd/index.html

23. Ibid.
24. Ibid.
25. IRC chat conversation between the author and Ana Voog, December 15, 2002.
26. Over the last five years, a number of Web market ratings companies such as Jupiter's Media Metrix have positioned themselves as "objective measurers" of site traffic. Yet rather than counting uniques, these companies operate in a similar way to television's Nielsen ratings, extrapolating overall trends from the preferences of a self-selected few Web surfers. See http://www.jup.com/bin/home.pl (viewed August 28, 2006).
27. Simon Firth, "Live! From My Bedroom!" Available online at http://archive.salon.com/21st/feature/1998/01/cov_08feature.html (viewed August 22, 2006).
28. IRC conversation with Jodi Anderson, business manager for Jennifer Ringley, October 22, 2001.
29. Nor do I know how many people artificially inflated this page view figure by keeping Ringley's camera image refreshing every five minutes on their computer desktop all day. This too is a common way hits become inflated on webcam sites.
30. The estimate of Ana Voog's daily viewership comes from the author's interviews with Voog.
31. Tila Tequila's MySpace page is located at http://www.myspace.com/tilatequila. See TMZ Staff, "Tila Tequila's 1.7 Million Friends Not Giving Single a Shot." TMZ. March 16, 2007. http://www.tmz.com/2007/03/16/tila-tequilas-1-7-million-friends-not-giving-single-a-shot/ (viewed September 1, 2007).
32. For a balanced analysis of MySpace and the music industry, see Adam Webb, "Making a Song and Dance." *The Guardian Online*, Thursday May 25, 2006 http://arts.guardian.co.uk/netmusic/story/0,,1782621,00.html.
33. Max Horkheimer and Theodor W. Adorno, *Dialectic of Enlightenment* (New York: Continuum, 1999).
34. Momus's LiveJournal is at http://www.livejournal.com/momus.
35. Dyer Quoted in, Stars P. David Marshall, *Celebrity and Power: Fame in Contemporary Culture* (Minneapolis: University of Minnesota Press, 1997), 17.
36. P. David Marshall, *Celebrity and Power: Fame in Contemporary Culture* (Minneapolis: University of Minnesota Press, 1997).
37. Jodi Dean, *Publicity's Secret*, 124.
38. Hugo Liu, "Social Network Profiles as Taste Performances," *Journal of Computer-Mediated Communication* 13.1 (2007). Available online at http://jcmc.indiana.edu/vol13/issue1/liu.html.
39. Thomas Frank, *The Conquest of Cool* (New York: University of Chicago Press, 1997).
40. Douglas B. Holt, *Cultural Branding* (Boston: Harvard Business School Press, 2004).
41. See http://www.tridentgum.com.
42. The Suicide Girls site is located at http://www.suicidegirls.com.
43. Virginia Heffernan and Tom Zeller Jr., "The Lonelygirl That Really Wasn't," *New York Times.* September 13, 2006.
44. Ibid.
45. Virginia Heffernan, "Applause for Lonely Girl15, and DVD Extras," *The Medium: A New York Times Blog.* Available online at http://themedium.blogs.nytimes.com/2006/ 09/12/lonely-girl-and-friends-just-wanted-movie-deal/ (viewed September 12, 2006).
46. Ibid.
47. Ibid.
48. Ibid.

49. Jean Baudrillard, *The Gulf War Did Not Take Place* (New York: Power Publications, 2004).

50. Wiliam E. Connolly, "Film Technique and Micropolitics," *Theory & Event* 6.1 (2002): 3–4.

Chapter 2

1. Atomcam existed at http://www.atomcam.com from 1999 to 2002. Stacy Pershall still maintains a mostly private online journal at http://www.livejournal.com/users/stacy (viewed August 28, 2006).

2. Planet Concrete existed at http://www.planetconcrete.com from 1998 to 2002. Eric's new site, Concrete 7, is available online at http://www.concrete7.com/ (viewed August 28, 2006).

3. The Web site for the South by Southwest Conference is at http://www.sxsw.com/ (viewed August 28, 2006).

4. Amandacam existed from 1998 to 2003 at http://www.amandacam.com (viewed November 22, 2002).

5. LiveJournal is available online at http://www.livejournal.com. My personal journal is available online at http://www.livejournal.com/users/tsenft (viewed August 28, 2006). My Friends List, where I read Allie's post, is available online at http://www.livejournal.com/users/tsenft/friends (viewed August 28, 2006).

6. In her defense, Allie claims to have tried to call us before posting her LiveJournal entry for public viewing.

7. Email interview with the author, August 2, 2001.

8. Sherry Turkle, *Life on the Screen: Identity in the Age of the Internet* (New York: Simon & Schuster, 1995).

9. See Lisa Nakamura, *Cybertypes: Race, Ethnicity, and Identity on the Internet* (New York: Routledge, 2002).

10. Judith P. Butler, *Bodies That Matter: On the Discursive Limits of "Sex"* (New York: Routledge, 1993).

11. Theresa Senft and Stacy Horn, ed. *Sexuality and Cyberspace: Performing the Digital Body*, Special issue of *Women and Performance: A Journal of Feminist Theory* 9.17 (1996). Available online at http://www.terrisenft.net/wp17/index.html (viewed August 28, 2006).

12. Kaley Davis and Theresa Senft, "Modem Butterfly, Reconsidered," *Sexuality & Cyberspace,* 69–104. Available online at http://www.terrisenft.net/wp17/senft_modem.html (viewed August 28, 2006).

13. Susan Leigh Star, *The Cultures of Computing, Sociological Review Monograph Series* (Oxford, UK, and Cambridge, MA: Blackwell, 1995).

14. See Susan C. Herring, *Computer-Mediated Communication: Linguistic, Social and Cross-Cultural Perspectives, Pragmatics & Beyond* (Philadelphia: J. Benjamins, 1996).

15. See, for example, Beth E. Kolko, Lisa Nakamura, and Gilbert B. Rodman, *Race in Cyberspace* (New York: Routledge, 2000).

16. Spivak and Rooney, "In a Word: Interview," 125.

17. Donna Haraway, "A Cyborg Manifesto: Science, Technology, and Socialist-Feminism, in the Late Twentieth Century," *Simians, Cyborgs and Women: The Reinvention of Nature* (New York: Routledge, 1991), 149–181. Available online at http://www.stanford.edu/dept/HPS/Haraway/CyborgManifesto.html (viewed August 26, 2006).

18. For an excellent history of cyborg-inspired 'cyberfeminism,' see Maria Fernandez and Faith Wilding, "Situating Cyberfeminism," in *Domain Errors! Cyberfeminist Practices*, eds. Faith Wilding, Michelle M. Wright, and Maria Fernandez (New York: Autonomedia, 2004).

19. Sharon Lehner, "My Womb, the Mosh Pit," *Women & Performance: A Journal of Feminist Theory. Special Issue: Sexuality and Cyberspace: Performing the Digital Body* 9.17 (1996): 179–186. Available online at http://www.terrisenft.net/wp17/lehner. html (viewed August 26, 2006).

20. See Allucquère Rosanne Stone, *The War of Desire and Technology at the Close of the Mechanical Age* (Cambridge, MA: MIT Press, 1995).

21. Bryan Alexander and Debra Deruyver, "Teresa (sic) Senft and Stacy Horn, editors, *Sexuality and Cyberspace: Performing the Digital Body* (Special issue of *Women & Performance: A Journal of Feminist Theory*, 1996." Resource Center for Cyberculture Studies, March 1999. Available online at http://www.com.washington.edu/rccs/ bookinfo.asp?ReviewID=43&BookID=42 (viewed August 28, 2006).

22. Jennifer Ringley's JenniCam, which existed from 1996 to 2004, was available online at http://www.jennicam.org (viewed August 22, 2003).

23. Email interview with the author, August 6, 2001.

24. Ana Voog, *Anatomy*. Available online at http://www.AnaCam.com/anatomy/ (viewed August 28, 2006). AnaCam, online since 1997, is available online at http:// www.AnaCam.com (viewed August 28, 2006).

25. For more on Fluxus, see Ken Friedman, *The Fluxus Reader* (Chichester, West Sussex, UK, and New York: Academy Editions, 1998). Synopsis available online at http:// www.nettime.org/nettime.w3archive/199901/msg00032.html (viewed March 22, 2003).

26. Ana Voog, *Anagram*. Available online at http://www.ana2.com/private/anagram/ anagram022199.html (viewed February 21, 2004).

27. Danni's Hard Drive, online since 1995, is at http://www.danni.com (viewed August 28, 2006).

28. Jacques Derrida, *Of Grammatology*, trans. Gayatri Spivak (Baltimore: Johns Hopkins Press, 1974), 49.

29. ArtVamp's site, online since 2001, is at http://www.artvamp.com (viewed August 28, 2006). Melissa Gira's "Beautiful Toxin" site, online since 2000, has moved to "Sacred Whore" at http://www.melissagira.com (viewed August 28, 2006).

30. http://www.webcamnow.com (viewed August 28, 2006).

31. http://www.citizenx.com (viewed August 28, 2006).

32. HereandNow was online from 1998 to 2002 at http://www.hereandnow.net (viewed October 7, 2001). Lisa Batey currently maintains a personal Web site at http://www. livejournal.com/users/lisagoddess (viewed August 28, 2006). Andrea Mignolo no longer maintains a web presence.

33. DefyMyCategory, begun in 1996, was available online at http://www.defymycategory. com. The site is now closed.

34. Sean Patrick Live, begun in 1996, was available online at http://www.seanpatricklive. com. The site is now closed.

35. Interview with the author, July 15, 2001. Eric's Planet Concrete Web site, which featured his webcam, was available online at http://www.planetconcrete.com. Eric's new site, Concrete 7, is available online at http://www.concrete7.com/ (viewed August 28, 2006).

36. From "Introduction," *Image Ethics in the Digital Age* (2003) Eds. Larry Gross, John Stuart Katz and Jay Ruby (Minnesota Press). Excerpt online at http://www.upress.umn.edu/excerpts/Gross.html.

37. Email interview with the author, July 7, 2001.

38. Email interview with the author, September 4, 2001.

39. SeeMeScreaming, which existed from 2000 to 2004, was at http://www.seemescreaming.com (viewed October 30, 2005).

40. Email interview with the author, August 7, 2001. Auriea Harvey's Web site is available online at http://e8z.org (viewed August 22, 2006).

41. Teresa Ditton and Matthew Lombard, "At the Heart of It All: The Concept of Telepresence," *Journal of Computer Mediated Communication* 3.2 (1997). Available online at http://jcmc.indiana.edu/vol3/issue2/lombard.html (viewed February 22, 2006).

42. HereandNow was online from 1998 to 2002 at http://www.hereandnow.net (viewed August 27, 2001). Andrea Mignolo no longer maintains a personal Web site.

43. Interview with the author, October 22, 2001.

44. Interview with the author, August 8, 2001.

45. *Diagnostic and Statistical Manual of Mental Disorders, Fourth Edition*, 2000. Available online at http://www.behavenet.com/capsules/disorders/voyeurismTR.htm (viewed October 3, 2001). For a contemporary treatment of the topic, see Jonathan Metzl, "Voyeur Nation? Changing Definitions of Voyeurism, 1950–2004," *Harvard Review of Psychiatry* 12 (2004): 127.

46. Laura Mulvey, "Visual Pleasure and Narrative Cinema," in *Feminism and Film Theory*, ed. Constance Penley (New York: Routledge, 1988), 57–68.

47. For her explanation of Mulvey's work, I am indebted to E. Ann Kaplan. See "Feminist Criticism and Television," in *Channels of Discourse, Reassembled: Television and Contemporary Criticism*, ed. Robert C. Allen (Chapel Hill, NC: University of North Carolina Press, 1992), 247–283.

48. Simon Firth, "Live! From My Bedroom!"

49. Email interview with author, January 24, 2002.

50. My idea of grabbing is meant to be Web-specific, predicated on the apparatus of new media delivery systems. For arguments that tactility be introduced to film theory, see Elena del Rio, "The Body of Voyeurism: Mapping a Discourse of the Senses in Michael Powell's Peeping Tom," *Camera Obscura* 15.3 (2000): 115.

51. Pew Internet Studies, "Wired Workers: Who They Are, What They are Doing Online" (September 3, 2000). Available online at http://www.pewinternet.org/reports/reports.asp?Report=20&Section=ReportLevel1&Field=Level1ID&ID=51 (viewed August 28, 2006).

52. See Karl Marx, "The Fetishism of the Commodity and Its Secret," in *Capital: A Critique of Political Economy,* Vol. 1 (New York: Penguin, 1905), 163. For a lucid explanation of the connections between fetishism in its sexual and commodity formations, see Linda Williams, *Hard Core: Power, Pleasure, and the "Frenzy of the Visible"* (Berkeley: University of California Press, 1999).

53. Robert Stoller, *Sexual Excitement: The Dynamics of Erotic Life* (New York: Pantheon Books, 1976), 6.

54. Karl Marx, "The Fetishism of the Commodity and Its Secret," in *Capital: A Critique of Political Economy,* Vol. 1 (New York: Penguin, 1905).

55. Ducky's webcam lasted from 2000 to 2003. Her Web site is now available online at http://duckydoolittle.com (viewed September 1, 2006).

56. Email interview with the author, June 3, 2001.

57. Roger Ebert, "Review: Live Nude Girls Unite," *Chicago Sun Times*, June 22, 2001. Avaialble online at http://www.livenudegirlsunite.com/ebert.html (viewed June 19, 2003).

58. Email correspondence with the author, April 19, 2001.

59. The Vera Little Media Project, begun in 2000, is available online at http://www. veralittle.com (viewed September 19, 2003).

60. Email interview with the author, May 7, 2001.

61. Trajectory Media is available online at http://www.trajectorymedia.com (viewed September 19, 2003).

62. Gavin Poynter, "Emotions in the Labour Process," *European Journal of Psychotherapy, Counseling & Health* 5.3 (2002): 247.

63. Gavin Poynter, "Emotions in the Labour Process," *European Journal of Psychotherapy, Counseling & Health* 5.3 (2002): 247.

64. Helaine Olen, "The New Nanny Diaries Are Online," *New York Times*, July 7, 2005.

65. Tassy, "Sorry to Disappoint You," Blogspot: Instructions to the Double. http://subvic.blogspot.com/2005/07/sorry-to-disappoint-you.html (viewed July 20, 2005).

66. See Spivak and Rooney, "In a Word: Interview," 124.

67. Ibid.

68. Laura M. Agustin, "A Migrant World of Services," *Social Politics: International Studies in Gender, State and Society* 10.3 (2004): 383.

Chapter 3

1. Ducky's site, online since 2000, is available online at http://www.duckydoolittle.com (viewed August 28, 2006). AnaCam, begun by Ana Voog 1997, is available online at http://www.AnaCam.com (viewed September 1, 2006). Stacy Pershall's Atomcam existed at http://www.atomcam.com from 1999 to 2002. Stacy Pershall still maintains a mostly private online journal at http://www.livejournal.com/users/stacy (viewed August 28, 2006).

2. Erving Goffman, *The Presentation of Self in Everyday Life* (New York: Doubleday, 1990).

3. Benjamin, "The Work of Art in the Age of Mechanical Reproduction," *Illumination* (New York: Schocken, 1968).

4. Baudrillard, *Simulations, Semiotext(E) Foreign Agents Series* (New York: Semiotext(e) Inc., 1983); Philip Auslander, *Liveness: Performance in a Mediatized Culture* (London and New York: Routledge, 1999).

5. Ditton and Lombard, "At the Heart of it All: The Concept of Telepresence."

6. Ibid.

7. Email interview with the author, August 7, 2001. Auriea Harvey's Web site is available online at http://e8z.org (viewed August 21, 2006).

8. Email interview with the author, November 2, 2001. ArtVamp's site is available online at http://www.artvamp.com (viewed August 28, 2006).

9. Ditton and Lombard, "At the Heart of it All," Concept Explication: 2. Presence as Realism.

10. Email interview with the author, August 2, 2001. Howie maintains a LiveJournal available online at http://www.livejournal.com/users/howief (viewed August 22, 2006).

11. Email interview with the author, August 2, 2001. HereandNow was online from 1998 to 2002 at http://www.hereandnow.net (viewed August 21, 2001). Lisa Batey currently maintains a personal Web site at http://www.lisagoddess.com (viewed August 22, 2003).
12. Instant message interview with the author, December 13, 2001. Maura Johnston's Web site is at http://www.maura.com (viewed August 22, 2006). Her LiveJournal is available online at http://www.livejournal.com/users/maura (viewed August 26, 2006).
13. Email interview with the author, November 11, 2001. Scott's LiveJournal site is located at http://www.livejournal.com/users/whorpool (viewed August 22, 2006).
14. Email interview with the author, November 3, 2001. Alan asked that his personal information not be given in this book.
15. Ibid.
16. Email interview with the author, July 3, 2001. Ira maintains a LiveJournal available online at http://www.livejournal.com/users/notwolf (viewed August 22, 2006).
17. Gerald Millerson, *The Technique of Television Production* (New York: Hastings House, 1969), 201–202. As cited in Ditton and Lombard, "At the Heart of it All."
18. Ditton and Lombard, "At the Heart of it All."
19. Email interview with the author, October 3, 2001.
20. Ibid.
21. Email interview with the author, July 2, 2001.
22. Ditton and Lombard, "At the Heart of it All."
23. Email interview with the author, November 7, 2001.
24. Ditton and Lombard, "At the Heart of it All," The notion of *presence as an actor* can also be used to understand the appeal of "virtual pets" (i.e., Tamaguchi) and the "virtual idol" phenomenon, as detailed in William Gibson's *Idoru* (New York: Viking Press, 1997). Indeed, when I originally began asking about "Net idols" in Japan (real women who run fan clubs off the Internet), I was often asked, "Do you also want to know about virtual idols, as well?" Some people even had trouble believing Net idols were living women in Japan, as their popularity is far overshadowed—in the American imagination at least—by their virtual counterparts.
25. Email interview with the author, May 3, 2001.
26. Hans Robert Jauss, "Literary History as a Challenge to Literary Theory," in *Toward an Aesthetic of Reception, Theory and History of Literature*, Vol. 2, ed. Hans Robert Jauss (Minneapolis: University of Minnesota Press, 1982), 18–36.
27. Email interview with the author, November 21, 2001.
28. Email interview with the author, July 7, 2001.
29. Email interview with the author, July 11, 2001. Magenta's webcam is available online at http://www.geocities.com/leanan_sidhe777/pagetwo.html (viewed August 22, 2001).
30. Email interview with the author, August 29, 2001.
31. Encyclopedia Dramatica is at http://www.encyclopediadramatica.com/.
32. Email interview with the author, August 25, 2001.
33. Jacques Derrida, *Of Grammatology*, 49. trans. Gayatri Spivak (Baltimore: Johns Hopkins Press, 1974), 49.
34. Ken Goldberg, *The Robot in the Garden. Telerobotics and Telepistemology in the Age of the Internet* (Cambridge, MA: MIT Press, 2000).
35. Ibid., 1.
36. Alan M. Turing, "Computing Machinery and Intelligence," *Mind* 54 (1950): 433–457.
37. Ibid.

38. N. Katherine Hayles, *How We Became Posthuman: Virtual Bodies in Cybernetics, Literature, and Informatics* (Chicago: University of Chicago Press, 1999), xi.
39. Jodi Dean, *Publicity's Secret*, 8.
40. At Karen's request, I have removed the drug names from this description.
41. I use Cameo's real name with her permission and at her request. I also respect her desire not to have her LiveJournal address published in this book.
42. This post was placed in the Friends Only part of Cameo's online journal.
43. I've copied the text for Cameo's parodies here with her permission. Another friend of Karen's from LiveJournal visited her in the hospital in subsequent days following the initial overdose, but I left Cameo's statement as is, lest anyone reading be confused. On the day I describe, I was the only one at the hospital. Additionally, I have chosen not to reprint Cameo's images here, since some LiveJournal members whose icons Cameo used might object to being called "guilty bystanders."
44. Elizabeth J. Donaldson, "The Corpus of the Madwoman: Toward a Feminist Disability Studies Theory of Embodiment and Mental Illness," *NWSA Journal* 14.3 (2003): 101.

Chapter 4

1. Walter M. Kendrick, *The Secret Museum: Pornography in Modern Culture* (New York: Viking, 1987).
2. This program was broadcast October 16, 2000 on National Public Radio, from 10 a.m. to 11 a.m. EST. Although I have omitted portions of the broadcast due to space concerns here, I have tried in my retelling to accurately represent the flow of the conversation. When I quote participants, it is from a transcript of the discussion I generated after listening to the entire show in Real Audio format on the Web at http://www.wamu.org/programs/dr/00/10/16.php (viewed August 22, 2006).
3. Jeffrey Rosen, *The Unwanted Gaze: The Destruction of Privacy in America* (New York: Random House, 2000).
4. SpotLife existed from 2000 to 2004 at http://www.spotlife.com (viewed August 22, 2003).
5. For a clear overview of Echelon, see Jane Perrone, "The Echelon Spy Network." *The Guardian,* May 29, 2001. Available online at http://www.guardian.co.uk/Archive/Article/0,4273,4194384,00.html (viewed August 9, 2006).
6. To better understand Carnivore/DCS1000, see the Electronic Privacy Information Center (EPIC's) article on Carnivore, http://www.epic.org/privacy/carnivore/ (viewed June 12, 2006).
7. Michael Warner, "Publics and Counterpublics," *Public Culture* 14.1 (2002): 49.
8. Ibid., 90.
9. Ibid., 89.
10. Habermas, Jürgen, *The Structural Transformation of the Public Sphere: An Inquiry into a Category of Bourgeois Society,* trans. Thomas Burger with Frederick Lawrence (Cambridge, MA: MIT Press, 1991).
11. Antje Gimmler, "Deliberative Democracy, the Public Sphere and the Internet," *Philosophy & Social Criticism* 27.4 (2001): 21–39.
12. Jodi Dean, *Publicity's Secret*, 157.
13. Carolyn J. Dean, "Empathy, Pornography, and Suffering," *Differences: A Journal of Feminist Cultural Studies* 14.1 (2003): 88–124.

14. Lauren Gail Berlant, *The Queen of America Goes to Washington City: Essays on Sex and Citizenship*, Series Q (Durham, NC: Duke University Press, 1997), 5.

15. Estimate according to Rick Muenynot of the YNOT Adult Network. See Nitya Jacob, "Free Adult Sites Are Bait for Pay Sites," *India Express*, June 6, 1999. Available online at http://www.expressindia.com/fe/daily/19990606/fle06021.html (viewed August 28, 2006). The YNOT network is located at http://www.ynotnetwork.com/ (viewed August 28, 2006).

16. Ibid.

17. Email interview with author, June 23, 2002.

18. Internet Friends Network (AKA iFriends) is at http://www.ifriends.com (viewed June 19, 2006).

19. Internet Friends Network Frequently Asked Questions. Online at http://apps7. ifriends.net/~wsapi/ifBrowse.dll?&filter=a (viewed June 19, 2003).

20. VoyeurDorm is online at http://www.voyeurdorm.com (viewed June 19, 2006).

21. Noah Schachtman, "VoyeurDorm: Address Unknown," *Wired News*, September 26, 2001. Available online at http://www.wired.com/news/politics/0,1283,47104,00. html (viewed June 19, 2006).

22. Ibid.

23. The Real House is available online at http://www.therealhouse.com (viewed September 19, 2003).

24. Email interview with the author, September 3, 2003.

25. Poynter, "Emotions in the Labour Process," *European Journal of Psychotherapy, Counselling & Health*.

26. Victoria Rideout, *Generation Rx.com: How Young People Use the Internet for Health Information*. Kaiser Family Foundation. December 2001. Online at http://www.kff. org/entmedia/20011211a-index.cfm (viewed August 28, 2006).

27. Nancy Fraser, "Rethinking the Public Sphere: A Contribution to the Critique of Actually Existing Democracy," in *Habermas and the Public Sphere*, ed. Craig J. Calhoun (Cambridge, MA: MIT Press, 1992).

28. Michael Warner, *Publics and Counterpublics* (New York, Cambridge, MA: Zone Books; distributed by MIT Press, 2002).

29. Stanley Milgram, *The Individual in a Social World: Essays and Experiments*, Second Edition, eds. Sabini and Silver (New York: McGraw-Hill, 1992).

30. Eric Paulos and Elizabeth Goodman, The Familiar Stranger: Anxiety, Comfort, and Play in Public Places. ACM SIGCHI Paper (April 2004) For more, see "The Familiar Stranger Project: Anxiety, Comfort and Play in Public Places." http://berkeley.intel-research.net/paulos/research/familiarstranger/index.htm (viewed August 28, 2006).

31. Pamela Robertson, *Guilty Pleasures: Feminist Camp from Mae West to Madonna* (Durham, NC: Duke University Press, 1996), 13.

32. Luce Irigaray, *Speculum of the Other Woman* (Ithaca, NY: Cornell University Press, 1985).

33. Email interview with the author, December 22, 2001. Melissa Gira's "Beautiful Toxin" site, online since 2000, has moved to http://www.melissagira.com (viewed June 19, 2006).

34. Douglas B. Holt, "Why Do Brands Cause Trouble? A Dialectical Theory of Consumer Culture and Branding," *Journal of Consumer Research* 29.1 (2002).

35. HereandNow was online from 1998–2002 at http://www.hereandnow.net (viewed June 22, 2001). Lisa Batey currently maintains a LiveJournal at http://livejournal. com/users/lisagoddess (viewed August 13, 2006).

36. The Stile Project is online at http://www.stileproject.com (viewed June 19, 2006).
37. This discussion can be read online at http://www.livejournal.com/talkread.bml?journal=ana&itemid=203584 (viewed June 19, 2003).
38. The images, and the conversation following, can be found on Ana Voog's LiveJournal at http://www.livejournal.com/talkread.bml?journal=ana&itemid=317456 (viewed June 19, 2003).
39. "The Red Flag" can be seen online at the Museum of Menstruation site at http://www.mum.org/armenjc.htm (viewed June 19, 2006).
40. Email interview with the author, July 27, 2001.
41. Quoted in Ana Voog's LiveJournal at http://www.livejournal.com/users/ana/318537.html (viewed June 19, 2003).
42. Ibid.
43. Of course, there are exceptions to this rule: people can and sometimes do decide to treat their LiveJournal as a one-way medium by turning off the comments feature. Friends Filters represent another technological 'fix' for a social dilemma. As a LiveJournal writer, I am asked before I send each post whether I want my words and images to be public, "Friends Only" (i.e., only viewable by those I have listed as friends), "Selected Friends Only," or private (i.e., only viewable by me). Other social networking services are developing friends filters similar to LiveJournal's.
44. Katherine Mieszkowski, "Candy from Strangers," *Salon*, August 13, 2002. Available online at http://www.salon.com/tech/feature/2001/08/13/cam_girls/print.html (viewed June 3, 2006).
45. James Kinkaid, *Erotic Innocence: The Culture of Child Molesting* (Durham: Duke University Press, 1998), 14.
46. Ibid., 13.
47. Steven Angelides, "Feminism, Child Sexual Abuse, and the Erasure of Child Sexuality," *GLQ: A Journal of Lesbian and Gay Studies* 10.2 (2004): 149.
48. "Two teens face child pornography charges," *The Associated Press*, March 29, 2006. Available online at http://www.boston.com/news/local/rhode_island/articles/2006/03/29/two_teens_face_child_pornography_charges/ (viewed July 2, 2006).
49. Philip Jenkins, *Beyond Tolerance: Child Pornography on the Internet* (New York: NYU Press, 2001).
50. Big Doggie exists at http://www.bigdoggie.net.
51. Jo Dozema, "Forced to Choose: Beyond the Voluntary V. Forced Prostitution Dichotomy," in *Global Sex Workers*, eds. Jo Dozema and Kamala Kempadoo (New York: Routledge, 1998), 39.
52. Montgomery, "Children, Prostitution, and Identity," 142.
53. Ibid.
54. See Ella Shohat, "Area Studies, Gender Studies, and the Cartographies of Knowledge," *Social Text* 20.3 (2002).
55. Email interview with the author, November 3, 2001.
56. Email interview with the author, November 15, 2001. Lux's LiveJournal is at http://www.livejournal.com/users/lux (viewed June 19, 2006).
57. Email correspondence with the author, September 3, 2000. Ira's LiveJournal is at http://www.livejournal.com/users/notwolf (viewed June 19, 2006).
58. Davies and Crabtree, "Invisible Villages: Technolocalism and Community Renewal."
59. Ibid.
60. Ibid.

Chapter 5

1. Robert Putnam, "Bowling Alone: America's Declining Social Capital," *Journal of Democracy* 6.1 (1995): 64–78. As Andy Blunden notes, Robert Putnam is not the first to write about social capital, and different theorists define the term differently: "Briefly, for Jane Jacobs [social capital] meant neighbourhood self-government; for Pierre Bourdieu it meant "distinction"; for James Coleman it means the power to control events in other people's lives; for Fukuyama it means "trust." Andy Blunden, "Social Solidarity Verus 'Social Capital':2: Capital" (Melbourne: Unpublished draft manuscript). Available online at http://home.mira.net/~andy/works/social-solidarity-2.htm (viewed August 22, 2004). For Jacobs on social capital, see *The Death and Life of Great American Cities* (New York: Random House, 1961). For Bourdieu, see *Distinction: A Social Critique of the Judgement of Taste* (Cambridge, MA: Harvard University Press, 1984). For Fukuyama, see *Trust: Social Virtues and the Creation of Prosperity* (New York: Free Press, 1995). For an excellent overview of social capital and online networks, see William Davies, *"You Don't Know Me, But ... Social Capital and Social Software"* (London: The Work Foundation, 2003). Available online at http://theworkfoundation.com/products/publications/azpublications/youdontknowmebutsocialcapitalandsocialsoftware.aspx (viewed November 22, 2006).

2. Huysman and Wolf quoted in Nicole Ellison, Charles Steinfield, and Chris Lampe, "Spatially Bounded Online Social Networks and Social Capital: The Role of Facebook." Talk given at the International Communications Association, 19–23, 2006, 1.

3. Putnam, "Bowling Alone: America's Declining Social Capital."

4. Barry Wellman, Anabel Quan-Haase, Jeffrey Boase, Wenhong Chang, et al. "The Social Affordances of the Internet for Networked Individualism," *Journal of Computer Mediated Communication* 8.3 (April 2003). Online at http://jcmc.indiana.edu/vol8/issue3/wellman.html.

5. eBay is located at http://www.ebay.com (viewed June 19, 2006). To see how the feedback system works, visit the Feedback Page at http://pages.ebay.com/services/forum/feedback.html.

6. Slashdot is located at http://www.slashdot.org (viewed June 19, 2006). For an explanation of the Slashdot "karma" system, see Frequently Asked Questions: Karma at http://slashdot.org/faq/com-mod.shtml#cm700.

7. Daily Kos is at http://www.dailykos.com. For an explanation of the ratings process, see the Daily Kos Frequently Asked Question: Rating Comments, at http://dkosopedia.com/wiki/DailyKos_FAQ#Rating_comments.

8. Andy Blunden, "Social Solidarity Versus 'Social Capital': Preface" (Melbourne: Unpublished draft manuscript, 2004). Available online at http://home.mira.net/~andy/works/social-solidarity-preface.htm (viewed September 13, 2004).

9. danah boyd, "Friends, friendsters, and Top 8: Writing community into being on social network sites," *First Monday* 11.12 (December 2006). Online at http://firstmonday.org/issues/issue11_12/boyd/index.html.

10. Kate Raynes-Goldie and David Fono, 2005. "Hyperfriendship and Beyond: Friendship and Social Norms on Livejournal," Association of Internet Researchers (AOIR-6), Chicago.

11. danah boyd, "Friends, friendsters, and Top 8: Writing community into being on social network sites," *First Monday* 11.12 (December 2006). Online at http://firstmonday.org/issues/issue11_12/boyd/index.html.

12. Benedict Anderson, *Imagined Communities: Reflections on the Origin and Spread of Nationalism* (New York: Verso, 2006).

13. The LiveJournal WeirdJews Community is at http://community.livejournal.com/weirdjews. To read the group's full profile, see http://community.livejournal.com/weirdjews/profile.

14. Correspondence with the author.

15. Susan Herring, Lois Ann Scheidt, Sabrina Bonus, and Elijah Wright. "Bridging the Gap: A Genre Analysis of Weblogs." Paper presented at the Thirty-Seventh Annual Hawaii International Conference on System Sciences (HICSS'04), Big Island, Hawaii, January 5, 2004. Online at http://www.ics.uci.edu/~jpd/classes/ics234cw04/herring.pdf (viewed June 2, 2006).

16. Ibid.

17. For more information, see the LiveJournal statistics page at http://www.livejournal.com/stats.bml.

18. Freud broke narcissism into two categories. The first—primary narcissism—happens in infants as a part of their developmental process. Freud saw the child's fascination with itself as a good thing and a way to ultimately separate from the mother. By contrast, Freud found secondary narcissism—the term he used for adults—dangerous. He argued that vain women and homosexuals constituted primary candidates for secondary narcissism because of their infantile self-absorption and preoccupation with their own image. See Sigmund Freud, "On Narcissism: An Introduction," *General Psychological Theory* (New York: Macmillan, 1963), 56–82.

19. Gayatri Chakravorty Spivak, "Echo," *New Literary History* 24.1 (1993): 14.

20. Thomas Bullfinch, *Bullfinch's Mythology* (New York: Kessinger Publishing, 2004), 88.

21. Spivak, "Echo," 14.

22. Email correspondence with the author, July 6, 2003. Trista's LiveJournal is at http://www.livejournal.com/users/trista (viewed June 19, 2006).

23. To read this entry online, see ArtVamp's LiveJournal at http://www.livejournal.com/users/artvamp/day/2002/08/23 (viewed August 1, 2006).

24. Email conversation with the author, August 25, 2002. Whorpool's LiveJournal is located at http://www.livejournal.com/users/whorlpool (viewed March 3, 2006).

25. Email conversation with the author, August 26, 2002. Laura's LiveJournal is located at http://www.livejournal.com/users/slit (viewed June 3, 2006).

26. Jodi Dean, *Solidarity of Strangers: Feminism after Identity Politics* (Berkeley: University of California Press, 1996), 13.

27. Ibid.

28. Jodi Dean, *Solidarity of Strangers,* 14.

29. Blunden, "Social Solidarity Versus 'Social Capital': Preface," n.p.

30. Anjum asked that her LiveJournal address not be published.

31. See http://thehomelessguy.wordpress.com/.

32. Email communication with the author, July 5, 2003.

33. Audrey Macklin, "'Our Sisters from Stable Countries': War, Globalization, and Accountability," *Social Politics: International Studies in Gender, State and Society* 10.2 (2003): 256–283.

34. Ibid., 272.

35. Ibid.

36. Ibid.

37. Ibid., 276.

38. Ibid.
39. Ibid., 276.
40. Ibid., 275.

Conclusion

1. Lawrence Lessig, *The Future of Ideas: The Fate of the Commons in a Connected World* (New York: Random House, 2001), 5.
2. Haraway, "A Cyborg Manifesto," in *Simians, Cyborgs, and Women: The Reinvention of Nature* (New York: Routledge, 1991).
3. Berlant, *The Queen of America Goes to Washington City: Essays on Sex and Citizenship, Series Q* (Durham, NC: Duke University Press, 1997).
4. Michael W. Apple, *Educating the "Right" Way: Markets, Standards, God, and Inequality* (New York: RoutledgeFalmer, 2001); Michael W. Apple, "Interrupting the Right: On Doing Critical Educational Work in Conservative Times," *Symploke* 10.1–2 (2002): 133–152; Michael W. Apple and Petter Aasen, *The State and the Politics of Knowledge* (New York and London: RoutledgeFalmer, 2003).
5. Correspondence with the author.
6. Connolly, "Film Technique and Micropolitics," 3–4.

Bibliography

Agustin, Laura M. "A Migrant World of Services." *Social Politics: International Studies in Gender, State and Society* 10.3 (2004): 377–396.

Alexander, Bryan, and Debra Deruyver. "Teresa [sic] Senft and Stacy Horn, editors, *Sexuality and Cyberspace: Performing the Digital Body*. Special issue of *Women & Performance: A Journal of Feminist Theory*, 1996. Resource Center for Cyberculture Studies, March 1999." <http://www.com.washington.edu/rccs/bookinfo.asp?ReviewID=43&BookID=42> (viewed August 28, 2006).

Anderson, Benedict. *Imagined Communities*. New York: Verso. 2006.

Angelides, Steven. "Feminism, Child Sexual Abuse, and the Erasure of Child Sexuality." *GLQ: A Journal of Lesbian and Gay Studies* 10.2 (2004): 141–177.

Apple, Michael W. *Educating the "Right" Way: Markets, Standards, God, and Inequality*. New York: RoutledgeFalmer, 2001.

———. "Interrupting the Right: On Doing Critical Educational Work in Conservative Times." *Symploke* 10.1–2 (2002): 133–152.

Apple, Michael W., and Petter Aasen. *The State and the Politics of Knowledge*. New York and London: RoutledgeFalmer, 2003.

Auslander, Philip. *Liveness: Performance in a Mediatized Culture*. London and New York: Routledge, 1999.

Baudrillard, Jean. *Simulations, Semiotext(E)*. *Foreign Agents Series*. New York: Semiotext(e) Inc., 1983.

———. *The Gulf War Did Not Take Place*. New York: Power Publications, 2004.

Benjamin, Walter. "Surrealism: The Last Snapshot of the European Intelligentsia." In *Reflections: Essays, Aphorisms, Autobiographical Writings*, xliii, 348. New York: Harcourt Brace Jovanovich, 1978.

———. "The Work of Art in the Age of Mechanical Reproduction." In *Illumination*. New York: Schocken, 1968:217–252.

Berlant, Lauren Gail. *The Queen of America Goes to Washington City: Essays on Sex and Citizenship*. *Series Q*. Durham: Duke University Press, 1997.

Blunden, Andy. "Social Solidarity versus 'Social Capital': Preface." Melbourne, Draft manuscript, 2004. <http://home.mira.net/~deller/ethicalpolitics/reviews/social-solidarity-preface.htm> (viewed September 15, 2006).

———. "Social Solidarity versus Social Capital." Paper presented at the Capacity Building and Community Strengthening Forum, University of Melbourne, July 13, 2004. <http://home.mira.net/~andy/works/public-policy.htm> (viewed September 13, 2006).

———. "Social Solidarity versus 'Social Capital': 2: Capital." Melbourne, Draft Manuscript, 2004. <http://home.mira.net/~deller/ethicalpolitics/reviews/social-solidarity-2.htm> viewed August 22, 2006).

Bourdieu, Pierre. *Distinction: A Social Critique of the Judgment of Taste.* Cambridge, MA: Harvard University Press, 1984.

boyd, danah and Nicole Ellison. "Social network sites: Definition, history, and scholarship." Journal of Computer-Mediated Communication, 13(1), article 11 (2007). Online at <http://jcmc.indiana.edu/vol13/issue1/boyd.ellison.html> viewed March 3, 2008.

boyd, danah. "Friends, friendsters, and Top 8: Writing community into being on social network sites," *First Monday* Volume 11, number 12 (December 2006). <http://firstmonday.org/issues/issue11_12/boyd/index.html> viewed 3 March 2007.

Butler, Judith P. *Bodies That Matter: On the Discursive Limits of "Sex."* New York: Routledge, 1993.

Castells, Manuel. *The Power of Identity.* Malden, MA: Blackwell, 1997.

———. The Information Age: Economy, Society and Culture, Volume 1: The Rise of the Network Society. Cambridge, MA: Blackwell Publishers, 1996.

Coleman, J. S., III. "The Creation and Destruction of Social Capital: Implications for the Law." *Journal of Law, Ethics, and Public Policy* 3 (1988): 375–404.

Connolly, William E. "Film Technique and Micropolitics." *Theory & Event* 6.1 (2002): 55–72.

Davies, William, and James Crabtree. "Invisible Villages: Technolocalism and Community Renewal." *Renewal: A Journal of Labour Politics* 12.1 (2004). <http://www.renewal.org.uk/issues/2004%20Voulme%2012/Invisible%20Villages.htm> (viewed April 1, 2006).

———. "You Don't Know Me, But … Social Capital and Social Software." Edited by iSociety. London: The Work Foundation, 2003. <http://www.theworkfoundation.com/products/publications/azpublications/youdontknowmebutsocialcapitaland-socialsoftware.aspx> (viewed November 22, 2006).

Davis, Kaley, and Theresa Senft. "Modem Butterfly, Reconsidered." *Women & Performance: A Journal of Feminist Theory. Special Issue: Sexuality & Cyberspace: Performing the Digital Body* 9.17 (1996): 69–104. <http://www.terrisenft.net/wp17/senft_modem.html> (viewed August 28, 2006).

Dean, Carolyn J. "Empathy, Pornography, and Suffering." *differences: A Journal of Feminist Cultural Studies* 14.1 (2003): 88–124.

Dean, Jodi. "Feminism in Technoculture." Paper presented at the Feminist Millennium Conference, University of Bergen, Norway, 2000. <http://people.hws.edu/dean/fem_tech.html> (viewed June 6, 2006).

———. "Introduction: Siting/Citing/Sighting the New Democracy." In *Feminism and the New Democracy,* edited by Jodi Dean. London: Sage, 1997: 1–21.

———. *Publicity's Secret: How Technoculture Capitalizes on Democracy.* Ithaca, NY: Cornell University Press, 2002.

del Rio, Elena. "The Body of Voyeurism: Mapping a Discourse of the Senses in Michael Powell's *Peeping Tom.*" *Camera Obscura* 15.3 (2000): 115–141.

Derrida, Jacques. *Of Grammatology.* Translated by Gayatri Spivak. Baltimore, MD: Johns Hopkins Press, 1974.

Ditton, Teresa, and Matthew Lombard. "At the Heart of It All: The Concept of Telepresence." *Journal of Computer Mediated Communications* 3.2 (1997). <http://jcmc.indiana.edu/vol3/issue2/lombard.html> (viewed February 22, 2006).

Donaldson, Elizabeth J. "The Corpus of the Madwoman: Toward a Feminist Disability Studies Theory of Embodiment and Mental Illness." *NWSA Journal* 14.3 (2003): 99–119.

Dozema, Jo. "Forced to Choose: Beyond the Voluntary V. Forced Prostitution Dichotomy." In *Global Sex Workers*, edited by Jo Dozema and Kamala Kempadoo, 39–50. New York: Routledge, 1998.

Duncombe, Stephen. Notes from Underground: Zines and the Politics of Alternative Culture. New York: Verso, 1997

Eco, Umberto Eco. *Travels in Hyperreality*. New York: Harcourt Press, 1990.

Felski, Rita. *Beyond Feminist Aesthetics: Feminist Literature and Social Change*. Cambridge, MA: Harvard University Press, 1989.

Fernandez, Maria and Wilding, Faith, "Situating Cyberfeminism," in *Domain Errors! Cyberfeminist Practices*, ed. Faith Wilding, Michelle M. Wright, and Maria Fernandez. New York: Autonomedia, 2004.

Thomas Frank, *The Conquest of Cool*. New York: University of Chicago Press, 1997.

Fraser, Nancy. "Rethinking the Public Sphere: A Contribution to the Critique of Actually Existing Democracy." In *Habermas and the Public Sphere*, edited by Craig J Calhoun. Cambridge, MA: MIT Press, 1992: 109–142.

Freud, Sigmund. "On Narcissism: An Introduction." *General Psychological Theory*. New York: Macmillan, 1963: 56–82.

Fukuyama, Francis. *Trust: Social Virtues and the Creation of Prosperity*. New York: Free Press, 1995.

Gimmler, Antje. "Deliberative Democracy, the Public Sphere and the Internet." *Philosophy & Social Criticism* 27, No. 4, (2001) 21–39.

Goffman, Erving. *The Presentation of Self in Everyday Life*. New York: Doubleday, 1990.

Goldberg, Ken. *The Robot in the Garden: Telerobotics and Telepistemology in the Age of the Internet*. Cambridge, MA: MIT Press, 2000.

Grandey, Alicia A. "Emotion in the Workplace: A New Way to Conceptualize Emotional Labor." *Journal of Occupational Health Psychology*. Vol. 5, No. 1 (2000) 95–110.

Gross, Larry, et al. "Introduction," *Image Ethics in the Digital Age* Eds. Larry Gross, John Stuart Katz and Jay Ruby. Minnesota Press, 2003. http://www.upress.umn.edu/excerpts/Gross.html (viewed March 1, 2008).

Habermas, Jürgen. *The Structural Transformation of the Public Sphere: An Inquiry into a Category of Bourgeois Society*. Trans. Thomas Burger with Frederick Lawrence. Cambridge, MA: MIT Press, 1991.

Hochschild, Arlie Russell. *The Managed Heart: Commercialization of Human Feeling*. Berkeley, CA: University of California Press, 1983.

Hanish, Carol, "The Personal Is Political" in *Notes from the Second Year: Women's Liberation*. Shulamith Firestone and Anne Koedt, Eds. (New York: Firestone and Koedt, 1970), 204–205.

———. "Updated Introduction to the Personal is Political." *Second Wave and Beyond*. Alexander Street Press. <http://scholar.alexanderstreet.com/pages/viewpage.action?pageId=2259> (viewed July 1, 2006).

Haraway, Donna. "A Cyborg Manifesto." In *Simians, Cyborgs, and Women: The Reinvention of Nature*, 149–181. New York: Routledge, 1991. <http://www.stanford.edu/dept/HPS/Haraway/CyborgManifesto.html> (viewed August 28, 2006).

Hayles, N. Katherine. *How We Became Posthuman: Virtual Bodies in Cybernetics, Literature, and Informatics*. Chicago: University of Chicago Press, 1999.

Herring, Susan, Lois Ann Scheidt, Sabrina Bonus, and Elijah Wright. "Bridging the Gap: A Genre Analysis of Weblogs." Paper presented at the Thirty-Seventh Annual Hawaii

International Conference on System Sciences (HICSS'04), Big Island, Hawaii, January 5, 2004. <http://www.ics.uci.edu/~jpd/classes/ics234cw04/herring.pdf> (viewed June 2, 2006).

Herring, Susan. *Computer-Mediated Communication: Linguistic, Social and Cross-Cultural Perspectives, Pragmatics & Beyond*. Philadelphia: J. Benjamins, 1996.

Holt, Douglas B. *Cultural Branding*. Boston: Harvard Business School Press, 2004.

————. "Why Do Brands Cause Trouble? A Dialectical Theory of Consumer Culture and Branding." *Journal of Consumer Research* 29.1 (2002): 70–90.

Horkheimer, Max, and Theodor W. Adorno. *Dialectic of Enlightenment*. New York: Continuum, 1999.

Hu-DeHart, Evelyn. "Globalization and Its Discontents: Exposing the Underside." *Frontiers: A Journal of Women Studies* 24.2 (2004): 244–260.

Hughes, Robert. The Shock of the New: Art and the Century of Change Lodon: Thames & Hudson, 1991.

Irigaray, Luce. *Speculum of the Other Woman*. Ithaca, NY: Cornell University Press, 1985.

Jacobs, Jane. *The Death and Life of Great American Cities*. New York: Random House, 1961.

Jauss, Hans Robert. *Toward an Aesthetic of Reception, Theory and History of Literature* Vol. 2. Minneapolis: University of Minnesota Press, 1982.

Jenkins, Philip. Beyond Tolerance: Child Pornography on the Internet. New York: NYU Press, 2001.

Kaplan, E. Ann. "Feminist Criticism and Television." In *Channels of Discourse, Reassembled: Television and Contemporary Criticism*, edited by Robert C. Allen. Chapel Hill: University of North Carolina Press, 1992:247–283. Kelley, Tim, Michael Minges, and Vanessa Grey.

Kempadoo, Kamala. "Introduction: Globalizing Sex Workers' Rights." In *Global Sex Workers: Rights, Resistance, and Redefinition*, edited by Kamala Kempadoo and Jo Dozema, 1–27. New York: Routledge, 1998.

Kendrick, Walter M. *The Secret Museum: Pornography in Modern Culture*. New York: Viking, 1987.

Kinkaid, James. *Erotic Innocence: The Culture of Child Molesting*. Durham: Duke University Press, 1998.

Kolko, Beth E., Lisa Nakamura, and Gilbert B. Rodman. *Race in Cyberspace*. New York: Routledge, 2000.

Lehner, Sharon. "My Womb, the Mosh Pit." *Sexuality and Cyberspace: A Journal of Feminist Theory. Special Issue: Sexuality and Cyberspace: Performing the Digital Body* 9.17 (1996): 179–186. <http://www.terrisenft.net/wp17/index.html> (viewed August 26, 2006).

Lessig, Lawrence. *The Future of Ideas: The Fate of the Commons in a Connected World*. New York: Random House, 2001.

Liu, Hugo. "Social network profiles as taste performances." *Journal of Computer-Mediated Communication*, 13(1), article 13 (2007) <http://jcmc.indiana.edu/vol13/issue1/liu.html> (viewed March 1, 2008).

Macklin, Audrey. "'Our Sisters from Stable Countries': War, Globalization, and Accountability." *Social Politics: International Studies in Gender, State and Society* 10.2 (2003): 256–283.

Marshall, P. David. *Celebrity and Power: Fame in Contemporary Culture*. Minneapolis: University of Minnesota Press, 1997.

Marx, Karl. "The Fetishism of the Commodity and Its Secret." In *Capital: A Critique of Political Economy*, Vol. 1, 163–177. New York: Penguin, 1905.

Metzl, Jonathan. "Voyeur Nation? Changing Definitions of Voyeurism, 1950–2004." *Harvard Review of Psychiatry* 12 (2004): 127–131.

Mieszkowski, Katherine. "Candy from Strangers." *Salon*, August 13, 2002, n.p. <http://www.salon.com/tech/feature/2001/08/13/cam_girls/print.html> (viewed June 3, 2006).

Milgram, Stanley. *The Individual in a Social World: Essays and Experiments.* Second Edition, eds. Sabini and Silver. New York: McGraw-Hill, 1992.

Millerson, G. *The Technique of Television Production.* New York: Hastings House, 1969.

Mohanty, Chandra. "'Under Western Eyes' Revisited: Feminist Solidarity through Anticapitalist Struggles." *Signs* 28.2 (2003): 499–525.

Montgomery, Heather. "Children, Prostitution and Identity: A Case Study from a Tourist Resort in Thailand." In *Global Sex Workers: Rights, Resistance, and Redefinition*, edited by Kamala Kempadoo and Jo Dozema, 139–150. New York: Routledge, 1998.

Mulvey, Laura. "Visual Pleasure and Narrative Cinema." In *Feminism and Film Theory*, edited by Constance Penley, 57–68. New York: Routledge, 1988.

Nakamura, Lisa. *Cybertypes: Race, Ethnicity, and Identity on the Internet.* New York: Routledge, 2002.

Paulos, Eric and Elizabeth Goodman, "The Familiar Stranger: Anxiety, Comfort, and Play in Public Places." Paper delivered at ACM SIGCHI (April 2004.) <http://berkeley.intel-research.net/paulos/research/familiarstranger/index.htm> (viewed August 28, 2006.)

Pew Internet Research Center. "Asian-Americans and the Internet: The Young and the Connected." Washington, D.C.: Pew Internet Group, 2001. <http://www.pewinternet.org/reports/reports.asp?Report=52&Section=ReportLevel2&Field=Level2ID&ID=345> (viewed August 28, 2006).

———. "Tracking Online Life: How Women Use the Internet to Cultivate Relationships with Family and Friends." Pew Internet Group, 2000. <http://www.pewinternet.org/reports/toc.asp?Report=11> (viewed August 28, 2006).

———. "Wired Workers: Who They Are, What They Are Doing Online." <http://www.pewinternet.org/reports/reports.asp?Report=20&Section=ReportLevel1&Field-Level1ID&ID=51> (viewed August 28, 2006).

Poynter, Gavin. "Emotions in the Labour Process," *European Journal of Psychotherapy, Counselling & Health,* 5.3 (2002): 110–124.

Putnam, Robert. "Bowling Alone: America's Declining Social Capital." *Journal of Democracy* 6.1 (1995): 64–78.

Raha, Maria. Cinderella's Big Score: Women of the Punk and Indie Underground. Seal Press 2004.

Raynes-Goldie, Kate and David Fono. "Hyperfriendship and Beyond: Friendship and Social Norms on Livejournal," Paper delivered at the Association of Internet Researchers (AOIR-6), Chicago, 2005.

Rheingold, Howard. *Smart Mobs: The Next Social Revolution.* Cambridge, MA: Perseus Publishing, 2002.

Rideout, Victoria. *Generation Rx.com: How Young People Use the Internet for Health Information.* Kaiser Family Foundation. December 2001. <http://www.kff.org/entmedia/20011211a-index.cfm> (viewed August 28, 2006.)

Robertson, Pamela. *Guilty Pleasures: Feminist Camp from Mae West to Madonna.* Durham, NC: Duke University Press, 1996.

Rosen, Jeffrey. *The Unwanted Gaze: The Destruction of Privacy in America.* New York: Random House, 2000.

Senft, Theresa M., and Stacy Horn (eds.). *Women and Performance: A Journal of Feminist Theory. Special Issue: Sexuality and Cyberspace: Performing the Digital Body* 9.17 (1996). <http://www.terrisenft.net/wp17/index.html> (viewed January 22, 2006).

———. "Performing the Digital Body: A Ghost Story." *Women and Performance: A Journal of Feminist Theory. Special Issue: Sexuality and Cyberspace: Performing the Digital Body* 9.17 (1996): 9–33. <http://www.terrisenft.net/wp17/intro.html> (viewed August 22, 2006).

Sharpe, Jenny, and Gayatri Chakravorty Spivak. "A Conversation with Gayatri Chakravorty Spivak: Politics and the Imagination." *Signs* 28.2 (2003): 609–27.

Shohat, Ella. "Area Studies, Gender Studies, and the Cartographies of Knowledge." *Social Text* 20.3 (2002): 67–78.

———. "Area Studies, Transnationalism, and the Feminist Production of Knowledge." *Signs* 26.4 (2001): 1269–1276.

Stoller, Robert. *Sexual Excitement: The Dynamics of Erotic Life* (1976) New York: Pantheon Books, 1976.

Star, Susan Leigh *The Cultures of Computing, Sociological Review Monograph Series* Oxford, UK, and Cambridge, MA: Blackwell, 1995.

Spivak, Gayatri Chakravorty. "Echo." *New Literary History* 24.1 (1993): 17–45.

———. "More on Power/Knowledge." In *Outside in the Teaching Machine*. New York: Routledge, 1993. 15–52

Spivak, Gayatri Chakravorty, and Ellen Rooney. "In a Word: Interview." *Differences: A Journal of Feminist Cultural Studies* 1.2 (1989): 124–156.

Stafford-Fraser, Quentin. "The Trojan Coffee Pot Timeline." <http://www.cl.cam.ac.uk/coffee/qsf/timeline.html> (viewed August 28, 2006).

Stone, Allucquère Rosanne. *The War of Desire and Technology at the Close of the Mechanical Age*. Cambridge, MA: MIT Press, 1995.

Turing, Alan M. "Computing Machinery and Intelligence." *Mind* 54 (1950): 433–457.

Turkle, Sherry. *Life on the Screen: Identity in the Age of the Internet*. New York: Simon & Schuster, 1995.

———. *The Second Self: Computers and the Human Spirit*. New York: Simon and Schuster, 1984.

Voskuil, Lynn M. "Feeling Public: Sensation Theater, Commodity Culture, and the Victorian Public Sphere." *Victorian Studies* 44.2 (2002): 245–274.

Wagenaar, Hendrik, and Maarten Hajer. "Introduction." In *Deliberative Policy Analysis: Understanding Governance in the Network Society*. Cambridge: Cambridge University Press, 2003: 5–34.

Warner, Michael. *Publics and Counterpublics*. New York, Cambridge, MA: Zone Books; distributed by MIT Press, 2002.

———. "Publics and Counterpublics." *Public Culture* 14.1 (2002): 49–90.

Wellman, Barry. "Computer Networks As Social Networks." *Science* 293 (2001): 2031–2034.

Index